I dedicate this book to my biggest
supporter and wife, Yoko, who
encouraged me to compile and
publish my thoughts, even if it
was just 'for my own good'.

And to all of my cats for giving
me the cuddles and healing, no
matter what day of the week.

February 22, 2022

Please share with your family and friends, especially
the younger generation so they can start growing early
(if children and young adults read Chapter 4 and begin
investing early on, they will have a great chance at
becoming millionaires, and gain many more options in
life).

CONTENTS

INTRODUCTION

Written by a self-made millionaire, now realizing that it is possible to become one in less than 20 years.

To reach what each of us consider success, it takes setting a clear goal as early as possible, taking small, realistic steps at a time, and continuing to keep an open mind until reaching our goal.

Each page in this book is meant to provide insights and options for you to choose toward your success.

To anyone looking for options to be independent (relief from financial stress; relief from work related stress).

To everyone looking for self-awareness and continuous improvement.

Photo Credit: NPS/Patrick Myers
Great Sand Dunes National Park - Mosca, Colorado

DUST TO MOUNTAIN

As we grow older, many of us begin searching for purpose and happiness in one way or another.

Based on my personal experience, and progress I have made in my life, I would like to use this platform to share my ideas for continued personal growth, sense of purpose, and happiness.

They are constant reminders to myself, which continues to help me realize in so many ways, that 'dust' accumulated makes a 'mountain'.

These ideas lead to my core mindset, which has allowed me to achieve success in various aspects of my life, including financial independence, and gaining the option of early retirement.

My favorite Japanese proverb:

Chirimo tsumoreba yamatonaru
(Dust accumulated makes a mountain)
– unknown author

This can be interpreted and used in a positive or a negative sense.

Positive interpretation would be something like: Consistent small efforts eventually leading to great accomplishments.

Negative interpretation would be something like: Continuing to ignore minor issues easily addressable, eventually leading to major problems that cannot be reversed.

There are so many areas this proverb may be applied to: personal, professional, physical, psychological, financial, environmental...

I will not assume that the ideas I list in this book directly applies to everyone.

I understand there are countless ways of achieving and interpreting 'success'.

They are ideas that I believe helped me along the way to my success, up to this point, and will continue to provide me with options to be happy, wherever I am in life.

Chapters 1 to 3 detail my philosophies / mindset, that has consistently allowed me to achieve my goals.

Chapter 4 lists tips on investing, which helped me to reach financial independence.

Chapters 5 to 7 detail what I believe to be some of the personality traits required (and ones to avoid) to be positively successful at work, and in life.

My hope is that, at least some of the items I mention will add to options for you to consider, in the path to what you determine to be your success.

CHAPTER 1: MY PHILOSOPHY / PURPOSE (FROM MY 20S)

My biggest motivation in life (both personal and professional) is to be relied upon; to be the "go-to person" in anything I do.

For this objective, I will continue to seek to improve myself, always being observant of the surrounding needs.

With this purpose, I continue to be motivated in everyting I choose to pursue.

By continuing to strive for this goal, I benefit myself by never seizing to gain knowledge and skills in everything I do, benefiting others with my support in the process, which in effect allows me to gain the greatest confidence and satisfaction in all that I accomplish.

Virtuous Cycle:

1) Motivation to improve lead to efforts to gain additional knowledge and skills.

2) Greater knowledge and skills lead to increase in reliability (increased ability to support others, as well as self-reliability).

3) Increase in ability to support others lead to greater confidence and satisfaction in everything I do.

4) All of the above lead to continued motivation to improve.

5) Back to 1).

With the goal of becoming the presence to be relied upon, in everything I pursue, along with my philosophy / mindset below, I will continue to improve, succeed, and move forward in life.

I try to keep an open mind, and attempt to see from the perspectives of others.

This is the first step to respecting and understanding, which is the first step to being respected and understood.

I won't "forget the past", but will not dwell on it either.

To dwell on the past, is to waste time and energy.

The only time things 'could have been', is after it 'has been', and I know I cannot turn back time.

"Everything happens for a reason."

I assess the experience, build a positive knowledge / energy from whatever happens, and guide myself to focus my time and effort toward a better future.

Some say "carpe diem" (i.e. live every moment as if it were the last).

I will, but only with a plan in place for tomorrow's success.

Thinking ahead, while being flexible in the paths toward my goals, is what will allow me to continue to "seize the day" in the days to come.

The only time I take things personally is when I feel that it will improve me in some way.

If I ever get 'offended' by something, I tell myself that I 'chose to care' enough about it, and it tells me I have room for growth (in the way I think, the way I carry myself, etc.).

No matter the topic in discussion, I will not dismiss anything as being "cliché" or "obvious".

There may be a good reason why some comments are made more than others, and any situation that requires 'overused' statements to be used, requires additional consideration to continue to improve going forward.

Rather than attempting to 'change' the world, I will attempt to change / improve myself... and see how it will 'influence' the world around me.

The key to happiness is to find a purpose in life to be passionate about... or to at least continue the search.

Whatever happens, as long as I am working toward some good purpose, I will keep a positive mind.

"Chirimo tsumoreba yamatonaru"
(Dust accumulated makes a mountain)

The more I think about this
proverb, the more it applies to
everything I can think of.

Good or bad, never ignore the 'dust',
no matter how small it may be.

If I disregard any little bad 'dust' I see, it
could eventually grow to be a 'mountain'
of problems that will hold me back.

If I appreciate and respect every little
good 'dust' around me, they will grow to
be a 'mountain' of positive motivation /
inspiration to carry me through.

Time / Energy / Money
– Save whenever possible,
to spend where it counts.

If assumption is a key to failure, open communication is the key to success.

Without it, one can only assume. Through it, one begins to understand.

People can communicate without being open, and this leaves room for assumption (i.e. belief without observation / analysis / understanding), which often lead to misunderstanding / confusion / conflict.

I will not live by assumptions or second hand knowledge / rumors.

I will live by the facts that I find first hand, and continue to observe with an open mind.

Now in my 40s, it makes me proud of what I wrote above in my 20s, and how I was able to compose myself to start off in the path to success.

Knowing my outcome up to this point, my hope is that everyone, at any age, will take and apply at least some pieces of this book with an open mind, to start building their positive 'mountain'.

One more quote below, which inspired me when I read it for the first time in my 20s (clicked with my emotion at the time):

"Once you fly, you will walk with your eyes skyward.

For there you have been, and there you will go again."

-- Leonardo da Vinci

CHAPTER 2: MY PHILOSOPHY / PURPOSE (FROM MY 40S)

One's purpose, and definition of living life to the fullest, will almost certainly be different things to each individual.

And it will most likely evolve over time at various phases in life.

When somebody once asked me, "what is your purpose?", I thought about it for a while, but I could not find a good answer at that particular moment (at the time, I had forgotten about what I wrote in Chapter 1).

If someone asked you "what is your purpose?", will you be able to answer?

The following day, I realized that I did not have to overthink it.

My current philosophy / purpose in life (in my 40s) is, quite simply, to continue searching for ways 'to be happy'.

In the most basic sense, I believe this is the honest purpose for most people.

For me, one way to be happy is to have financial independence.

To have enough money to live comfortably for the rest of my life, with the freedom to do whatever I choose to do (travel, check off my bucket list, completely relax, eat and learn to cook a variety of delicious food, experiment new ways to stay healthy, be a positive influence and help others, volunteer, etc.), all without having to worry about my financial future.

And in my path to financial independence, I consciously reminded myself that every effort and every savings (Time, Energy, Money) counts toward my happiness.

Of course, no matter how much money you have, good health and safety are essential to being happy.

As with growing wealth, growing a healthy body and mind also takes accumulation of many efforts, such as regular exercise, eating healthy, and positive thinking.

Also, as with growing wealth, you need to be able to identify any risks that may exist, and continue to manage them.

But once you build up to financial independence, while considering all of the risks involved, you gain many options to cover other necessities to be healthy, safe, and ultimately happy, without having to stress over the finance.

I am not implying that everyone will be unhappy without financial independence.

I am speaking from my own experience, that financial independence will provide more options to be happy.

Occasionally, I hear about wealthy people taking their own lives, and it confirms that "money can't buy happiness" for everyone.

There is no way to know exactly what those individuals were going through, but there must have been many negative 'dust' not being addressed, until they grew too big to overcome.

It is definitely an unfortunate situation to think about, but at least those individuals had 'more options' to be happy, in their own way, without having to worry about money.

The message here is that, although money can't always buy happiness, with financial independence, you are definitely gaining more options to consider toward happiness, while minimizing / eliminating financial stress.

And if you follow the overall message of this book, you will gain a positive mindset to address any negative 'dust' early on, to be able to put yourself in a better situation.

When I think about my purpose in life, I think about what I am usually doing each day -- in my personal life, and in my professional life (this section was written when I turned 40, before early retirement).

On weekdays / workdays, I:

- Wake up
- Get ready for work
- Go to work
- Go home for lunch and take a nap
- Go back to work
- Get back home to enjoy the rest of the day with my family
- Go to sleep
- and repeat

On weekends / non-workdays, I:

- Wake up
- Feed the cats
- Take care of personal projects
- Take a nap
- Go grocery shopping for the next week with my wife
- Go on other errands
- Get back home to enjoy the rest of the day with my family
- Go to sleep
- and repeat

Of course, there are some days where I go outside of usual routine, like going out after work to run errands, take some days off from work to relax, vacation, do other projects at home, watch movies, go to events, eat out, etc.

I am not trying to make my life sound overly simplified or boring.

But for the most part, the basic daily routine for weekdays and weekends remain the same.

Here, I am being honest with myself, listing the actual daily routine to better understand how I view my usual daily life as is, and to see where each daily action fits into my purpose in life, which is to be happy.

I suggest everyone to try listing your daily routine, in order to have a better perspective of your life, and to see how it fits with your current purpose.

Be completely honest with yourself, as this is also an important step, where you are identifying your positive and negative 'dust'.

In my case, without thinking about adding other activities to the list above, I see that everything except one word on the list fits my purpose to be happy.

The one word that does not fit my purpose 'to be happy' is, 'work'.

I understand that different individuals think of work differently.

Some people are blessed to consider work as part of their passion, where they may find their work to be their purpose in life, and their source of happiness.

For me, work is not my passion.

It is simply a source of income and benefits, such as insurance, 401k, HSA, etc., to cover my life expenses.

If there are other options to cover living expenses now and for the rest of my life, without having to work, if it were not for some satisfying reasons such as to help others grow and improve, etc., I will not be going to work every weekday (occasionally even on weekends and evenings).

Every time I hear or read about somebody I know who suddenly passed away due to a heart attack, cancer, coronavirus, etc., when they were just about to retire from work after over 30 years at a company, or when they were still young with so many things they wanted to accomplish, I think of myself and how I want to live the rest of my life.

I do not want to keep working until my end, unless I find work that I can consider my passion in life.

To be happy, I needed to achieve financial independence early, so I get to choose whether or not I want to work.

If I chose to continue working, I will choose work that will simply make me happy in life (which includes the satisfaction gained from helping others), and not because I need the income to live.

Luckily, I had been on the correct path to financial independence since my high school years, when I started getting curious about **investing** (Chapter 4).

Back then, I had no money, no reason to think about financial independence, and no reason to even imagine that I could retire a millionaire in my 40s.

It was the open-mindedness that helped me stay curious, and each small step brought me closer to realizing the 'dream' as it came to be.

Through trial and error, persistence, patience, and flexibility, now looking back, I had always been on my path to fulfill my purpose in life, 'to be happy'.

This is where the saying, "dust accumulated makes a mountain" also comes into play.

What is your purpose?

_____

_____

_____

List of Routine Activities (Does not have to be in any order)	Fit your purpose? (Y / N)

If "Y", think of ways to further improve the output.
If "N", think of ways to address/eliminate, with a clear target.

CHAPTER 3: MINDSET

Even at a young age, I practiced building a positive mindset, knowing it was a benefit to myself, and kept progressing in the direction toward achieving what I consider to be an overall success.

I believe this positive mindset came from various interactions, especially in childhood, such as learning early from my parents and grandparents to appreciate, respect, and to realize the value of everything I encounter (not necessarily directly or verbally, but more through their actions and examples), including the appreciation and respect for the value of money, which ultimately provided me with the flexibility to pursue many options toward a fulfilling life.

Appreciating and respecting everything I encounter, and the constant curiosity and drive to understand the value of everything I encounter, allows me to remain open-minded.

This in effect allows me to absorb various ideas and suggestions I read or hear, where I realize that by doing so, I am benefiting myself by gaining multiple options I may not have thought of myself, allowing me to choose the ideas and suggestions that I consider will improve my ways of thinking, and add value to my approach toward various things.

I always tell myself that this is easier said than done, and by constantly realizing this, I remind myself to continue striving to remain open-minded.

An open mind allows you to observe and listen to advice from others without resistance or assumption, where again, you benefit yourself by gaining additional options to choose what you feel will add value, and apply those to your current situation, for your ongoing growth.

Even with many positive interactions coming your way, if you tend to start by looking for something to criticize with a narrow perspective, you become close-minded and may miss out on potentially good ideas being presented, possibly losing many opportunities to gain new options to consider to supplement your 'great ideas' (in this case, you are starting to build a negative 'mountain').

Open-mindedness allows you to take a step back and view from various perspectives, avoiding skewed decisions, for an increased chance at supporting others, and improving yourself.

This trait has helped me to succeed, both personally and professionally.

In communicating with others, in various troubleshooting to resolve concerns efficiently and effectively, in supporting and guiding others with insights, as well as openly receiving support and guidance from others as appropriate, etc.

In addition, I was able to apply this trait to continue researching and developing an investment strategy that works for my risk tolerance, leading myself to early financial independence.

Just to be clear, having an open mind is just the first step in working toward achieving various goals.

There are a few other things to consider in order to reach success, such as:

- Setting clear / realistic goals, milestones, and priorities.

- Actually putting in the extra effort to make consistent progress.

- Understanding and utilizing available resources and support.

- Constantly improving and implementing ideas after thoughtful considerations.

- Always taking ownership / accountability in everything you choose to do.

Rather than simply taking ideas or suggestions that others provide, expand on the options you chose for yourself, and incorporate into your own ideas to apply to your own situation and objective.

The mindset / philosophies I describe above, along with additional ideas I list in the next few pages, allowed me to achieve many success, including financial independence, which provided me the option of early retirement.

And achieving financial independence gives me additional options to pursue whatever I choose to do for the rest of my life, still within my means, also considering potential changes in my lifestyle over time.

I recommend everyone to pursue at least part of this path to gain more options in life.

The earlier you start identifying and accumulating the positive 'dust' in your life (also to identify and address the negative 'dust' to prevent from growing), the sooner and bigger the 'mountain' will become.

My original goal was simply to be able to live a comfortable middle class life for the rest of my life.

I was never seriously thinking about early retirement, until around my 15th year of investing, when I began to notice that my annual compounding growth was increasing exponentially, as my accounts grew larger over time.

Because I took action early on, to take the first step with an open mind, I was able to reach and exceed my original goal earlier than I could have imagined at the time I started.

With the correct mindset, investment strategy, and some time, I believe anyone can achieve the goal of financial independence, and I am proof of concept.

Just set a goal, and continue moving forward.

CHAPTER 4: INVESTING

I started investing in the stock market on my 21st birthday, less than 2 months before 9/11/2001.

Since then, I experienced the market sell-off and recession following 9/11, the great recession of 2008, bankruptcies of companies I invested in, flash crash and several other market selloffs / corrections, various geopolitical concerns, 2020 worldwide downturn with increased volatility due to the COVID-19 pandemic and fear of severe inflation that followed, and many indecisions and mistakes in between.

Even with so many negative events along the way, through many ups and downs over 20 years or so, with a modest but consistent investment strategy, considering all of what I list in the next few pages in mind, I was able to become a millionaire before my 41st birthday.

One of the best method to speed up the financial growth (to reach financial independence), is through investing in the stock market and taking advantage of compounding interest.

There is a lot more to investing than what I share in this chapter, such as research, strategy, individual risk and emotional tolerance / management, etc.

The idea is to realize that, **even pennies, accumulated over time, have the potential to grow into hundreds of thousands of dollars**.

Please share these ideas with your loved ones, as early in their lives as possible, and even consider investing for growing generational wealth.

Take your first step as early as possible, knowing that it is never too late to start.

Even if you have already started investing, there is always more to learn, and always room to refine your approach.

Table below lists items I considered in my path to financial independence:

(IMPORTANT: READ EACH ITEM CAREFULLY)

Roth / Traditional 401k / IRA, HSA (invest in as many of these as you can, as much as possible, **after you secure your living expense and emergency fund**)	Choose between Pre-Tax or Post-Tax money to invest. Roth (investing post-tax money) is good, since investment gain is not taxed when you become eligible to take money out (because you are investing money that was already taxed). Traditional (investing pre-tax money) is also good, depending on where you are in the tax bracket, and if investing pre-tax money from your paycheck will lower your income tax.
Determine risk level (adjust with age and phases in life)	Aggressive (higher risk / 'growth') / Moderate (medium risk) / Conservative (lower risk / 'value')
Realize the potential risks in investing	There are always some risks in investing; **only invest money you do not need for emergencies.**
Determine both short-term and long-term target	Are you an investor (buy and hold for a long period) or a trader (buy and sell quickly)? Set respective target for each case.

Stocks / Bonds / Index Funds / ETFs / Commodity / Real Estate / etc.	Decide on the type of investment (for starters, **Index Funds** are most recommended/balanced).
Keep with funds that have **low expense ratio** (whatever rate the expense ratio is, that's how much you are giving away to the fund managing company; the larger your portfolio grows, the more you give away based on expense ratio)	Expense ratio is a fee that certain investment funds charge to manage the fund. Higher expense ratio can have a negative impact to your investment growth. **(Example: even if you have a 0.5% dividend paying fund, if expense ratio is 1.0%, you are giving away all of the dividend plus additional 0.5% to the fund).** Unless your risk level accepts growth funds that charge higher expense ratio, try to keep with funds that have expense ratio well below 0.5%.
Study the investment options (**only invest in what you know**)	Know what you are investing in, and although you do not want to have to constantly monitor your investment (assuming you invest in what you can be confident in), you need to **keep up with current events that may affect your investment.**

Check historical data / trend	Evaluate how the stocks / funds have performed over time using past data, and look for good companies that have a lot of cash, good customer satisfaction and reputation, pricing power, future potential and/or high dividend yield. **Realize that historical performance of a company or fund does not guarantee future performance.**
Decide on a budget	Whether short term or long term, decide how much to invest in each investment you choose, and stick with it. **Don't let emotion take over to go outside of your initial budget.** Re-evaluate your risk level, and study the investment carefully before making any decision to revise a budget.
Be sure to select / register your investment choice in your investment account after funding (unlikely mistake, but possible)	It's possible to fund the account without selecting any investment. Until the investment selection is made, the money will just sit in the account as cash without being invested.

Diversify your investment (but don't over-diversify) - "barbell strategy" to be able to reallocate / rotate when necessary (based on current events)	Invest in multiple sectors (tech, financial, health, industrial, energy, etc.) rather than all in a single sector. This is to reduce risk of overexposure to any one sector, because if you invest in a single sector that goes down at a certain time, your entire account goes down, but if you invest in multiple sectors where one does bad but others do good, you can constantly consider **reallocation / rebalancing,** so your overall investment will be positive long term. However if you over-diversify, where you are in too many sectors or companies, you increase the risk of exposing your account to more negative performing sectors than positive ones at any given time. This is also why it is very important to study each investment, and current events, so you have better chances of choosing better investments at various timeframes.

Cost averaging over time ("dollar cost averaging")	One option is to make investments in fractions, purchasing the same investment in multiple sections (rather than buying in all at once). Especially when the market is volatile, or has been in a long bull market, if you are worried about a bubble bursting right after you start investing, divide your total budget by a half, a third, or a quarter. Whatever you are comfortable with even if the market goes down after your initial purchase. And go ahead and purchase that initial fraction amount now, see how it performs in the next few weeks or months, and decide whether or not to buy more of the same investment if it goes down, or even if it's worth adding when it goes up from your initial purchase cost. In the long run, the overall base cost becomes your average overall purchase (so you don't risk buying everything at the 'high').

At a minimum, invest enough to receive the full company match in a 401k (as much as the company you work for offers)	If a company matches up to 6% of your investment into 401k each paycheck, you should at least invest 6% into your 401k to **take full advantage of the maximum company match**.
If possible, maximize your 401k investments as much as you feel comfortable, up to the amount currently allowed	Investment in 401k is pre-tax, so you are basically putting money into 401k without being taxed for that amount (you will be taxed when you take out money from your regular 401k; some companies offer Roth 401k, where investment gains are not taxed, same as Roth IRA).
Understand the power of compounding interest	A single investment doubles in value every 10 years at about 7.18% annual compounding interest.
Don't try to time the market	Nobody can predict the bottom (low point) or the peak (high point) in any investment, so there is no way to predict when is the "best time" to get in or out; this is why it is important to first come up with a plan and stick with it.

There are many good resources available for investment research and guidance. (**Study cyclical / secular trends of the market, current events and ideas, etc.**)	CNBC Acorns.com Charles Schwab Yahoo Finance Google etc.
Whenever you have any questions or concerns about investing and financial planning, consult a CFP (Certified Financial Planner)	Each individual financial situation is different, and not all ideas / suggestions in this book will apply directly to everyone. **If you are not fully confident in your own investment strategy, consult a CFP.**
After you have considered all of the above, don't hesitate and invest NOW (there's always a risk of markets going down, but **you have to be in it to enjoy the potential for future growth**)	Considering everything mentioned above, go ahead and invest TODAY. **5, 10, 20 years from now, the current fluctuation in price will not matter much, if at all. Even if the market crashes tomorrow, 5, 10, 20 years from now, as long as you keep due diligence investing in the market, your account will be worth much more than when you started investing (very likely, it will be worth much more much sooner than 5, 10, or 20 years).**

In investing, there will be times where the entire stock market tumbles over, whether due to economic downturn / recession, over-inflation, Fed interest rate hikes, geopolitical uncertainties, or any other fear inducing unknowns.

As long as you check off each of the items listed in the table above, keeping with your well thought-out plan while adjusting with the phases of your life, and avoiding emotionally rash decisions, you will progress past those temporary bumps, and your investments should continue to grow over time.

Always prepare for the worst, keep investable cash on hand, and consider any pullbacks as option to make additional investments for the future.

When you experience a market crash, tell yourself, "now I have the option to average down on my cost basis, for what I consider as a good long term investment; it would be much harder to add on over the years, if the price just continued to increase".

As an exaggerated example, say you purchased 1 share of a company stock for $100 last year, and the overall market crashes this year to cause the stock price to fall by 50% to $50 a share.

If your latest research still shows the company has potential, and you are still confident in it as a long term investment, you could opt to purchase 1 more share for $50 a share, where you will now have 2 shares of the company stock for an average cost basis of $75 per share.

Changing the example above, if you had purchased the same stock at $50 a share last year, and purchased another share after it goes up 100% to $100 a share this year, the average cost basis of $75 will be the same.

The big difference between the two examples above is that it is much more difficult to purchase additional shares of a company stock that has gone up 100% in price, compared to something that went down by 50%, when the potential for future growth remains the same.

If you have a long term view (depends on each individual) in investing, and you complete proper research, while also following the table above as a guide, whether you buy higher now and lower later, or vice versa, your investments should continue to grow in the long run.

And again, it is much easier to average down than to average up, when you want to increase the total number of shares you invest in over time.

The point here is to not feel so bad even when your initial investment goes down, as long as you have done proper research and continue to dollar cost average for a long term investment.

To show that the timing of your investment does not matter too much long term, one study from Charles Schwab* compared performance of five hypothetical investors that invested $2,000 a year (less than $6/day) over 20 years ($40,000 total) between 2001 and 2020.

Investors ① to ④ invested in the S&P500 index fund, and investor ⑤ in U.S. Treasury bills for 20 years.

① Invested at the **lowest point** each year

② Invested on the **first trading day** each year

③ Divided $2,000 into **12 increments and invested at the beginning of the month for 12 months** each year

④ Invested at the **highest point** each year

⑤ Avoided the stock market and invested in the **U.S. Treasury bills** each year

* Reference of this study gathered from the Charles Schwab article below (by Schwab Center for Financial Research):

https://www.schwab.com/resource-center/insights/content/does-market-timing-work

After 20 years, although the portfolio value for investor ①, who was able to invest at the lowest point each year (practically impossible for any investor to achieve), unsurprisingly had the highest growth at $151,391, even investor ④, who invested at the highest point each year, was still able to grow the $40,000 total investment to more than triple, at $121,171.

Although the $30,000 difference is significant, this shows that even one of the worst-case investment scenario can grow significantly over time.

Just as reference, investor ② ended the 20 years with $135,471, investor ③ with $134,856, and only investor ⑤ who completely avoided the stock market ended up losing money after considering inflation, with $44,438.

Even if early retirement is not your goal, the idea is to be better off than not doing anything toward a more comfortable future.

Keeping in mind that there may be some years your account will decrease significantly in value, over time, the average annual growth in the S&P500 (benchmark index of overall U.S. stock market) from inception to 2021 has been around 7% compounding growth, even after adjusting for inflation.

The following table shows the power of compounding interest of a set amount of annual contribution (in this example, Roth IRA max contribution limit in 2021; $6000 a year; less than $17/day) over 37 years invested, showing the difference of growth over the years, depending on the percentage compounding.

You will see that even a fraction of this amount will be a great addition to your wealth.

	Higher Interest Bank or Treasury Bill			Investment in Stock Market (historical growth of S&P500 is around 7% after adjusting for inflation)						
Interest Rate (%)	1	2	3	4	5	6	7	8	9	10
Periodic Rate	0.01005	0.02020	0.03045	0.04081	0.05127	0.06183	0.07250	0.08328	0.09416	0.10516
Duration (Years)	$	$	$	$	$	$	$	$	$	$
1	6,000.00	6,000.00	6,000.00	6,000.00	6,000.00	6,000.00	6,000.00	6,000.00	6,000.00	6,000.00
2	12,060.30	12,121.20	12,182.72	12,244.85	12,307.60	12,370.99	12,435.01	12,499.67	12,564.97	12,630.93
3	18,181.51	18,366.06	18,553.72	18,744.54	18,938.59	19,135.90	19,336.56	19,540.61	19,748.12	19,959.15
4	24,364.23	24,737.07	25,118.74	25,509.48	25,909.52	26,319.10	26,738.48	27,167.90	27,607.64	28,057.97
5	30,609.09	31,236.78	31,883.69	32,550.49	33,237.84	33,946.44	34,677.04	35,430.38	36,207.24	37,008.43
6	36,916.71	37,867.79	38,854.65	39,878.82	40,941.86	42,045.40	43,191.16	44,380.93	45,616.59	46,900.08
7	43,287.73	44,632.75	46,037.91	47,506.22	49,040.84	50,645.12	52,322.56	54,076.87	55,911.94	57,831.89
8	49,722.77	51,534.36	53,439.91	55,444.87	57,555.04	59,776.57	62,116.00	64,580.26	67,176.73	69,913.25
9	56,222.49	58,575.40	61,067.33	63,707.49	66,505.75	69,472.64	72,619.47	75,958.35	79,502.24	83,265.03
10	62,787.52	65,758.67	68,927.03	72,307.30	75,915.33	79,768.22	83,884.45	88,283.98	92,988.34	98,020.83
11	69,418.54	73,087.04	77,026.08	81,258.05	85,807.32	90,700.40	95,966.16	101,636.05	107,744.32	114,328.29
12	76,116.20	80,563.46	85,371.78	90,574.07	96,206.44	102,308.52	108,923.80	116,100.05	123,889.76	132,350.57
13	82,881.17	88,190.90	93,971.63	100,270.26	107,138.71	114,634.39	122,820.88	131,768.58	141,555.48	152,268.00
14	89,714.13	95,972.43	102,833.37	110,362.14	118,631.44	127,722.38	137,725.52	148,741.95	160,884.65	174,279.86
15	96,615.76	103,911.14	111,964.98	120,865.85	130,713.38	141,619.63	153,710.75	167,128.82	182,033.89	198,606.39
16	103,586.75	112,010.23	121,374.68	131,798.21	143,414.73	156,376.15	170,854.93	187,046.90	205,174.60	225,491.00
17	110,627.80	120,272.93	131,070.94	143,176.69	156,767.24	172,045.10	189,242.08	208,623.72	230,494.28	255,202.69
18	117,739.61	128,702.53	141,062.47	155,019.52	170,804.30	188,682.87	208,962.32	231,997.39	258,198.11	288,038.73
19	124,922.90	137,302.42	151,358.29	167,345.63	185,561.01	206,349.38	230,112.29	257,317.57	288,510.60	324,327.66
20	132,178.38	146,076.04	161,967.64	180,174.76	201,074.26	225,108.23	252,795.66	284,746.35	321,677.38	364,432.59
21	139,506.77	155,026.89	172,900.08	193,527.42	217,382.84	245,026.97	277,123.60	314,459.34	357,967.21	408,754.79
22	146,908.82	164,158.55	184,165.46	207,424.98	234,527.51	266,177.31	303,215.33	346,646.75	397,674.17	457,737.72
23	154,385.26	173,474.69	195,773.89	221,889.68	252,551.15	288,635.40	331,198.74	381,514.65	441,120.02	511,871.48
24	161,936.83	182,979.01	207,735.85	236,944.66	271,498.81	312,482.11	361,210.97	419,286.26	488,656.83	571,697.73
25	169,564.30	192,675.33	220,062.08	252,614.02	291,417.88	337,803.28	393,399.12	460,203.40	540,669.81	637,815.05
26	177,268.43	202,567.52	232,763.69	268,922.81	312,358.14	364,690.10	427,920.95	504,528.03	597,580.43	710,884.99
27	185,049.98	212,659.54	245,852.11	285,897.15	334,371.96	393,239.37	464,945.64	552,543.89	659,849.89	791,638.66
28	192,909.74	222,955.43	259,339.10	303,564.18	357,514.38	423,553.88	504,654.65	604,558.41	727,982.77	880,884.04
29	200,848.49	233,459.31	273,236.83	321,952.18	381,843.24	455,742.77	547,242.61	660,904.56	802,531.19	979,514.09
30	208,867.02	244,175.37	287,557.78	341,090.56	407,419.39	489,921.94	592,918.24	721,943.09	884,099.25	1,088,515.66
31	216,966.14	255,107.90	302,314.85	361,009.95	434,306.76	526,214.46	641,905.39	788,064.76	973,347.93	1,208,979.37
32	225,146.66	266,261.28	317,521.33	381,742.23	462,572.58	564,750.99	694,444.17	859,692.88	1,071,000.46	1,342,110.54
33	233,409.39	277,639.96	333,190.89	403,320.55	492,287.52	605,670.28	750,792.05	937,286.01	1,177,848.16	1,489,241.23
34	241,755.16	289,248.51	349,337.64	425,779.45	523,525.87	649,119.67	811,225.21	1,021,340.92	1,294,756.87	1,651,843.55
35	250,184.80	301,091.55	365,976.11	449,154.87	556,365.73	695,255.59	876,039.84	1,112,395.71	1,422,673.95	1,831,544.45
36	258,699.17	313,173.84	383,121.28	473,484.21	590,889.21	744,244.15	945,553.59	1,211,033.32	1,562,635.98	2,030,141.94
37	267,299.10	325,500.19	400,788.57	498,806.38	627,182.62	796,261.74	1,020,107.15	1,317,885.24	1,715,777.14	2,249,623.10

Note: The table assumes flat annual $6000 contribution invested at the end of each 365 day/year; focus on how much and how significantly compounding interest can grow over time.

The chart in the following page is a plot of the table above, where you can clearly see the difference in growth of a 1-3% bank interest or treasury bill versus a higher compounding interest investment that increases exponentially.

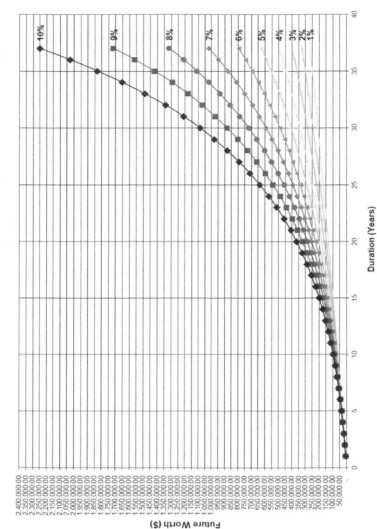

Compounding Interest Growth (Example: $6000 Annual Roth IRA Investment)

Note: One option available with Roth IRA, is that you can actively trade individual stocks (not just funds) within the account for any number of trades, without ever incurring capital gains tax (in a regular brokerage account, every gain from each trade is taxed), although you will not be able to use any losses for tax deduction as in a regular brokerage account.

If you are a young trader, not needing the money until age 59.5, you could opt to actively trade within a Roth IRA rather than in a regular brokerage account, to take advantage of potential increase in growth with the Roth tax advantage.

As with anything else in investing, this is just one option available to consider, but **for the average investor, a historically safer passive investing in low-cost index funds is always recommended over active trading in higher risk individual stocks**, especially for retirement accounts.

I also highly recommend you research HSA option, to also fully invest in early as possible.

Just like Roth IRA, earnings in HSA will not be taxed when you become eligible to withdraw, further supplementing your retirement.

I made the following 3 tables* more recently for my teenage nieces, to show how just a dollar, 50 cents, or even dime a day (increasing daily savings with multiples of age), will grow significantly over several years, demonstrating that "dust accumulated makes a mountain".

For example, if you were to start investing just a dime a day for a child when they turn 1 year old, in a fund that compounds 8% annually (which is historically realistic), continuing to invest a dime a day increasing multiples by their age each year, the investment will reach a million dollars by the time they are 66.

And this is not even considering any other savings / investments they will most likely add on over that timeframe.

*The tables assume 365 days/year; compounding growth calculation based on one time total investment for each year; focus on the power of compounding interest!

Dollar a day times age

Age	Annual (US$)	Monthly (US$)	Daily (US$)	Total Investment (US$)	Compounding +1%	Compounding +2%	Compounding +3%	Compounding +4%	Compounding +5%	Compounding +6%	Compounding +7%	Compounding +8%	Compounding +9%	Compounding +10%
1	365.00	30.42	1.00	365.00	368.65	372.30	375.95	379.60	383.25	386.90	390.55	394.20	397.85	401.50
2	730.00	60.83	2.00	1,095.00	1,109.64	1,124.35	1,139.13	1,153.98	1,168.91	1,183.91	1,198.99	1,214.14	1,229.36	1,244.65
3	1,095.00	91.25	3.00	2,190.00	2,228.68	2,263.73	2,301.15	2,338.94	2,377.11	2,415.65	2,454.57	2,493.87	2,533.55	2,573.62
4	1,460.00	121.67	4.00	3,650.00	3,723.55	3,798.21	3,873.99	3,950.90	4,028.96	4,108.19	4,188.59	4,270.18	4,352.97	4,436.98
5	1,825.00	152.08	5.00	5,475.00	5,604.04	5,735.62	5,869.96	6,006.94	6,146.66	6,289.18	6,434.54	6,582.79	6,733.99	6,888.17
6	2,190.00	182.50	6.00	7,665.00	7,871.98	8,084.19	8,301.76	8,524.81	8,753.49	8,987.93	9,228.26	9,474.61	9,727.14	9,985.99
7	2,555.00	212.92	7.00	10,220.00	10,531.25	10,851.97	11,182.46	11,523.01	11,873.92	12,235.51	12,608.06	12,991.98	13,387.54	13,795.09
8	2,920.00	243.33	8.00	13,140.00	13,585.76	14,047.41	14,525.53	15,020.73	15,533.62	16,064.84	16,615.05	17,184.94	17,775.21	18,386.60
9	3,285.00	273.75	9.00	16,425.00	17,039.47	17,679.06	18,344.85	19,037.96	19,759.55	20,510.83	21,293.05	22,107.54	22,955.63	23,838.76
10	3,650.00	304.17	10.00	20,075.00	20,896.36	21,755.64	22,654.69	23,595.47	24,580.02	25,610.48	26,689.07	27,818.14	29,000.14	30,237.64
11	4,015.00	334.58	11.00	24,090.00	25,160.47	26,286.05	27,469.78	28,714.89	30,024.77	31,403.00	32,853.35	34,379.79	35,986.50	37,677.90
12	4,380.00	365.00	12.00	28,470.00	29,835.88	31,279.37	32,805.28	34,418.69	36,125.01	37,929.98	39,839.69	41,860.57	43,999.49	46,263.69
13	4,745.00	395.42	13.00	33,215.00	34,926.89	36,744.86	38,676.79	40,730.24	42,913.51	45,235.48	47,705.61	50,334.02	53,131.49	56,109.56
14	5,110.00	425.83	14.00	38,325.00	40,437.05	42,691.96	45,100.39	47,673.85	50,424.69	53,366.21	56,512.71	59,879.54	63,483.23	67,341.51
15	5,475.00	456.25	15.00	43,800.00	46,371.17	49,130.30	52,092.85	55,274.80	58,694.67	62,371.69	66,326.85	70,582.90	75,164.47	80,098.17
16	5,840.00	486.67	16.00	49,640.00	52,733.29	56,069.70	59,670.63	63,559.39	67,761.41	72,304.39	77,218.53	82,536.74	88,294.87	94,531.98
17	6,205.00	517.08	17.00	55,845.00	59,527.67	63,520.19	67,851.90	72,554.97	77,664.73	83,219.95	89,263.17	95,841.08	103,004.86	110,810.68
18	6,570.00	547.50	18.00	62,415.00	66,758.05	71,492.00	76,654.56	82,289.97	88,446.46	95,177.35	102,541.50	110,603.96	119,436.60	129,118.75
19	6,935.00	577.92	19.00	69,350.00	74,430.58	79,995.54	86,097.24	92,793.97	100,150.54	108,239.09	117,139.85	126,942.08	137,745.04	149,659.12
20	7,300.00	608.33	20.00	76,650.00	82,547.89	89,041.45	96,199.16	104,097.72	112,823.07	122,471.43	133,150.64	144,981.45	158,099.09	172,655.04
21	7,665.00	638.75	21.00	84,315.00	91,115.02	98,640.58	106,980.09	116,233.23	126,512.47	137,944.62	150,672.73	164,858.16	180,682.86	198,352.04
22	8,030.00	669.17	22.00	92,345.00	100,136.47	108,803.99	118,460.39	129,233.76	141,269.59	154,733.10	169,811.93	186,719.21	205,697.02	227,020.24
23	8,395.00	699.58	23.00	100,740.00	109,616.78	119,542.97	130,661.05	143,138.91	157,147.82	172,915.78	190,681.41	210,723.35	233,360.90	258,956.77
24	8,760.00	730.00	24.00	109,500.00	119,560.55	130,869.03	143,603.68	157,969.67	174,203.21	192,576.33	213,402.31	237,042.02	263,911.13	294,488.44
25	9,125.00	760.42	25.00	118,625.00	129,972.41	142,793.91	157,310.54	173,778.46	192,494.62	213,803.41	236,104.22	265,860.38	297,009.38	333,974.79
26	9,490.00	790.83	26.00	128,115.00	140,857.03	155,320.59	171,804.56	190,599.19	212,083.85	236,691.01	264,925.82	297,378.41	334,738.32	377,811.27
27	9,855.00	821.25	27.00	137,970.00	152,219.15	164,063.54	182,282.45	203,249.22	227,440.06	255,418.59	287,852.30	325,531.96	369,394.65	426,432.89
28	10,220.00	851.67	28.00	148,190.00	164,063.06	184,262.83	196,274.79	216,282.85	248,299.17	279,307.75	316,333.00	369,651.07	420,551.13	480,318.18
29	10,585.00	882.08	29.00	158,775.00	176,395.03	196,724.79	219,118.48	244,261.44	270,397.52	304,746.45	346,963.31	404,031.19	469,938.38	538,993.50
30	10,950.00	912.50	30.00	169,725.00	189,218.48	211,828.29	238,135.15	256,933.74	291,356.94	331,885.53	379,740.92	436,401.43	503,857.21	603,948.95
31	11,315.00	942.92	31.00	181,040.00	202,538.81	227,606.16	256,933.74	291,246.54	331,685.78	379,740.92	416,401.43	503,857.21	583,676.83	679,088.14
32	11,680.00	973.33	32.00	192,720.00	216,361.00	244,071.88	276,672.15	315,158.42	360,743.80	414,906.17	479,447.13	556,564.18	648,918.95	758,844.95
33	12,045.00	1,003.75	33.00	204,765.00	230,690.06	261,239.22	297,378.66	340,291.55	391,428.24	452,568.24	525,896.58	614,097.92	720,472.50	849,078.94
34	12,410.00	1,034.17	34.00	217,175.00	245,531.06	279,122.20	319,082.32	366,809.61	424,030.16	492,876.94	575,988.04	676,628.55	798,841.99	947,637.84
35	12,775.00	1,064.58	35.00	229,950.00	260,889.12	297,785.15	341,813.04	394,768.00	458,645.41	535,901.06	629,976.45	744,555.83	884,662.45	1,056,454.12
36	13,140.00	1,095.00	36.00	243,090.00	276,760.41	317,046.16	365,431.48	424,224.32	495,374.68	582,078.92	688,134.63	818,146.08	978,604.68	1,176,553.54
37	13,505.00	1,125.42	37.00	256,595.00	299,177.16	337,209.60	390,479.83	455,238.49	534,323.67	631,318.95	750,754.38	898,361.82	1,081,309.55	1,309,064.39
38	13,870.00	1,155.83	38.00	270,465.00	310,117.63	358,683.05	416,480.33	487,872.83	575,603.35	683,900.29	818,148.08	985,210.37	1,193,843.80	1,455,227.83
39	14,235.00	1,186.25	39.00	284,700.00	327,596.15	379,782.92	443,636.79	522,192.14	619,330.27	740,023.41	890,649.90	1,079,601.00	1,316,805.90	1,616,409.11
40	14,600.00	1,216.67	40.00	299,800.00	345,618.12	402,399.58	471,983.80	558,263.83	665,626.78	799,900.81	968,617.39	1,181,521.08	1,451,232.43	1,794,110.02
41	14,965.00	1,247.08	41.00	314,265.00	364,180.95	425,580.29	501,557.36	596,157.98	714,621.37	863,757.76	1,052,433.16	1,292,204.96	1,598,155.20	1,989,982.52
42	15,330.00	1,277.50	42.00	329,595.00	383,314.14	449,728.49	532,393.98	635,947.50	766,448.94	931,833.01	1,142,506.58	1,412,137.76	1,758,608.86	2,205,843.78
43	15,695.00	1,307.92	43.00	345,290.00	403,042.33	474,781.96	564,531.65	677,708.30	821,251.14	1,004,379.71	1,239,275.99	1,542,059.38	1,934,089.31	2,443,092.65
44	16,060.00	1,338.33	44.00	361,350.00	423,249.82	500,607.80	597,909.76	721,518.93	879,408.70	1,081,666.09	1,343,209.19	1,682,804.93	2,125,662.75	2,705,727.91
45	16,425.00	1,368.75	45.00	377,775.00	444,071.57	527,245.48	632,667.48	767,461.69	940,381.78	1,163,976.56	1,455,339.18	1,835,129.44	2,334,875.65	2,994,368.21
46	16,790.00	1,399.17	46.00	394,565.00	465,470.18	555,046.73	669,147.15	815,621.76	1,005,030.87	1,251,612.55	1,574,610.48	2,000,073.00	2,563,315.56	3,312,274.03
47	17,155.00	1,429.58	47.00	411,720.00	487,451.44	583,645.74	706,991.22	866,087.63	1,073,294.64	1,344,893.60	1,703,189.07	2,178,606.24	2,812,712.91	3,662,371.94
48	17,520.00	1,460.00	48.00	429,240.00	510,021.15	613,189.08	746,143.35	918,952.14	1,145,355.37	1,444,158.42	1,841,158.70	2,371,816.34	3,084,958.47	4,047,881.13
49	17,885.00	1,490.42	49.00	447,125.00	533,185.21	643,720.85	786,949.41	974,310.62	1,221,402.39	1,549,766.02	1,989,176.76	2,580,877.45	3,382,064.37	4,472,342.74
50	18,250.00	1,520.83	50.00	465,375.00	556,949.56	675,184.47	829,355.39	1,032,263.05	1,301,635.01	1,662,066.09	2,147,946.64	2,807,057.64	3,706,375.36	4,939,652.02
51	18,615.00	1,551.25	51.00	483,990.00	581,320.21	708,756.45	873,409.50	1,092,913.17	1,386,282.51	1,781,554.71	2,318,220.05	3,051,726.45	4,060,239.49	5,454,093.72
52	18,980.00	1,581.67	52.00	502,970.00	606,303.21	741,188.57	919,161.19	1,156,368.90	1,475,504.63	1,908,566.79	2,500,805.02	3,316,362.97	4,446,349.25	6,020,381.09
53	19,345.00	1,612.08	53.00	522,315.00	631,904.69	774,989.28	966,661.37	1,222,742.45	1,569,592.11	2,043,586.49	2,696,583.92	3,602,564.61	4,867,606.73	6,643,019.21
54	19,710.00	1,642.50	54.00	542,025.00	658,180.84	811,363.52	1,015,962.51	1,292,150.55	1,668,767.22	2,187,094.28	2,908,409.43	3,912,056.57	5,327,175.23	7,326,749.57
55	20,075.00	1,672.92	55.00	562,100.00	684,987.90	846,714.37	1,067,118.84	1,364,714.57	1,773,284.33	2,339,569.44	3,131,338.37	4,246,702.10	5,828,502.75	8,084,807.03
56	20,440.00	1,703.33	56.00	582,540.00	712,462.18	885,477.23	1,120,185.40	1,440,560.76	1,883,410.55	2,501,041.81	3,372,402.85	4,608,513.47	6,375,347.60	8,915,731.73
57	20,805.00	1,733.75	57.00	603,345.00	740,620.05	924,815.68	1,175,220.31	1,519,820.39	1,999,426.32	2,673,795.62	3,630,732.40	4,999,863.95	6,971,806.34	9,830,234.40
58	21,170.00	1,764.17	58.00	624,515.00	769,407.95	964,905.59	1,232,281.81	1,602,680.00	2,121,626.14	2,856,661.45	3,907,533.57	5,422,500.66	7,622,344.21	10,834,544.84
59	21,535.00	1,794.58	59.00	646,050.00	798,852.19	1,006,369.01	1,291,431.32	1,689,131.60	2,250,316.00	3,050,888.22	4,204,105.51	5,879,558.52	8,331,828.32	11,943,887.83
60	21,900.00	1,825.00	60.00	667,950.00	828,950.16	1,048,639.79	1,352,731.26	1,779,472.87	2,385,830.16	3,257,155.61	4,519,528.52	6,373,575.20	9,105,563.88	13,162,366.61
61	22,265.00	1,855.42	61.00	690,215.00	859,737.15	1,092,313.71	1,416,246.15	1,873,807.38	2,528,499.92	3,476,185.74	4,862,177.26	6,907,507.41	9,949,353.48	14,503,094.77
62	22,630.00	1,885.83	62.00	712,845.00	891,190.82	1,137,242.34	1,482,042.43	1,972,294.88	2,678,686.41	3,708,744.69	5,226,743.77	7,484,548.61	10,869,440.20	15,976,034.25
63	22,995.00	1,916.25	63.00	735,840.00	923,327.66	1,183,442.34	1,550,188.55	2,075,101.47	2,836,765.48	3,955,644.07	5,617,220.48	8,108,146.88	11,872,754.37	17,601,421.47
64	23,360.00	1,946.67	64.00	759,200.00	956,154.56	1,230,843.98	1,620,869.13	2,182,399.93	3,003,131.76	4,217,744.31	6,033,641.81	8,782,027.43	12,966,764.66	19,387,259.62
65	23,725.00	1,977.08	65.00	782,925.00	989,678.35	1,279,756.65	1,693,814.41	2,294,369.93	3,178,199.59	4,495,957.47	6,483,286.34	9,510,212.62	14,159,633.73	21,352,083.08
66	24,090.00	2,007.50	66.00	807,015.00	1,023,906.04	1,329,751.18	1,769,441.54	2,411,198.32	3,362,404.07	4,791,250.32	6,962,892.69	10,297,046.83	15,460,258.83	23,513,790.39
67	24,455.00	2,037.92	67.00	831,470.00	1,058,844.65	1,381,466.16	1,847,713.44	2,533,079.46	3,556,202.03	5,104,647.64	7,476,462.02	11,147,221.98	16,878,338.11	25,892,069.93
68	24,820.00	2,068.33	68.00	856,290.00	1,094,501.29	1,434,931.66	1,928,709.44	2,660,215.44	3,760,073.13	5,437,235.70	8,025,177.16	12,065,805.34	18,424,442.34	28,508,196.23
69	25,185.00	2,098.75	69.00	881,475.00	1,130,883.16	1,488,788.62	2,012,511.28	2,792,816.45	3,974,521.03	5,790,165.94	8,615,165.74	13,058,269.56	20,110,093.80	31,387,140.32
70	25,550.00	2,129.17	70.00	907,025.00	1,167,997.49	1,544,094.85	2,099,101.11	2,931,101.11	4,200,074.59	6,164,658.90	9,245,838.54	14,130,525.13	21,947,851.74	34,651,959.35
71	25,915.00	2,159.58	71.00	932,940.00	1,205,851.61	1,601,951.40	2,188,871.06	3,075,296.76	4,437,209.07	6,562,008.33	9,920,484.50	15,288,955.34	23,951,405.75	38,037,861.78
72	26,280.00	2,190.00	72.00	959,220.00	1,244,452.93	1,662,509.22	2,282,266.85	3,225,639.83	4,686,747.52	6,983,585.63	10,634,651.06	16,540,454.17	26,135,677.47	41,870,935.96
73	26,645.00	2,220.42	73.00	985,865.00	1,283,808.91	1,721,189.85	2,377,499.74	3,382,376.22	4,949,062.14	7,430,844.47	11,416,560.63	17,892,467.10	28,516,911.49	46,086,921.06
74	27,010.00	2,250.83	74.00	1,012,875.00	1,323,927.10	1,783,163.85	2,476,644.01	3,545,761.67	5,224,875.75	7,905,325.74	12,244,620.78	19,353,035.27	31,112,896.22	50,725,324.16
75	27,375.00	2,281.25	75.00	1,040,250.00	1,364,815.12	1,846,749.63	2,579,139.58	3,716,062.14	5,514,863.29	8,408,662.78	13,131,035.49	20,930,943.09	33,942,895.63	55,827,969.08

50 cents a day times age

Age	Annual (US$)	Monthly (US$)	Daily (US$)	Total Investment (US$)	Compounding +1%	Compounding +2%	Compounding +3%	Compounding +4%	Compounding +5%	Compounding +6%	Compounding +7%	Compounding +8%	Compounding +9%	Compounding +10%
1	182.50	15.21	0.50	182.50	184.33	186.15	187.98	189.80	191.63	193.45	195.28	197.10	198.93	200.75
2	365.00	30.42	1.00	547.50	554.82	562.17	569.56	576.99	584.46	591.96	599.49	607.07	614.68	622.33
3	547.50	45.63	1.50	1,095.00	1,113.34	1,131.87	1,150.58	1,169.47	1,188.55	1,207.82	1,227.28	1,246.93	1,266.77	1,286.81
4	730.00	60.83	2.00	1,825.00	1,861.77	1,899.10	1,936.99	1,975.45	2,014.48	2,054.09	2,094.29	2,135.09	2,176.48	2,218.49
5	912.50	76.04	2.50	2,737.50	2,802.02	2,867.84	2,934.98	3,003.47	3,073.33	3,144.59	3,217.27	3,291.40	3,366.99	3,444.09
6	1,095.00	91.25	3.00	3,832.50	3,935.99	4,042.09	4,150.88	4,262.41	4,376.75	4,493.96	4,614.13	4,737.31	4,863.57	4,993.00
7	1,277.50	106.46	3.50	5,110.00	5,265.62	5,425.98	5,591.23	5,761.50	5,936.96	6,117.75	6,304.04	6,495.99	6,693.77	6,897.55
8	1,460.00	121.67	4.00	6,570.00	6,792.88	7,023.70	7,262.77	7,510.36	7,766.81	8,032.42	8,307.53	8,592.47	8,887.61	9,193.30
9	1,642.50	136.88	4.50	8,212.50	8,519.73	8,839.53	9,172.42	9,518.98	9,879.77	10,255.41	10,646.53	11,053.77	11,477.82	11,919.38
10	1,825.00	152.08	5.00	10,037.50	10,448.18	10,877.82	11,327.35	11,797.74	12,290.01	12,805.24	13,344.53	13,909.07	14,500.07	15,118.82
11	2,007.50	167.29	5.50	12,045.00	12,580.24	13,143.03	13,734.89	14,357.45	15,012.39	15,701.50	16,426.68	17,189.90	17,993.25	18,838.95
12	2,190.00	182.50	6.00	14,235.00	14,917.94	15,639.69	16,402.64	17,209.34	18,062.51	18,964.99	19,919.84	20,930.29	21,999.74	23,131.84
13	2,372.50	197.71	6.50	16,607.50	17,463.34	18,372.43	19,338.39	20,365.12	21,456.76	22,617.74	23,852.81	25,167.01	26,565.75	28,054.78
14	2,555.00	212.92	7.00	19,162.50	20,218.53	21,345.98	22,550.19	23,836.92	25,212.34	26,683.11	28,256.35	29,939.77	31,741.61	33,670.78
15	2,737.50	228.13	7.50	21,900.00	23,185.59	24,565.15	26,046.33	27,637.40	29,347.34	31,185.84	33,163.42	35,291.45	37,582.23	40,049.08
16	2,920.00	243.33	8.00	24,820.00	26,366.64	28,034.85	29,835.32	31,779.70	33,880.70	36,152.19	38,609.26	41,268.37	44,147.44	47,265.99
17	3,102.50	258.54	8.50	27,922.50	29,763.83	31,760.10	33,925.95	36,277.48	38,832.36	41,609.97	44,631.59	47,920.54	51,502.43	55,405.34
18	3,285.00	273.75	9.00	31,207.50	33,379.32	35,746.00	38,327.28	41,144.98	44,223.23	47,588.67	51,270.75	55,301.98	59,718.30	64,559.37
19	3,467.50	288.96	9.50	34,675.00	37,215.29	39,997.77	43,048.62	46,396.98	50,075.27	54,119.54	58,569.93	63,471.04	68,872.52	74,829.56
20	3,650.00	304.17	10.00	38,325.00	41,273.94	44,520.72	48,099.58	52,048.86	56,411.53	61,235.72	66,575.32	72,490.72	79,049.55	86,327.52
21	3,832.50	319.38	10.50	42,157.50	45,557.51	49,320.29	53,490.04	58,116.62	63,256.23	68,972.31	75,336.37	82,429.00	90,341.43	99,176.02
22	4,015.00	334.58	11.00	46,172.50	50,068.23	54,402.00	59,230.19	64,616.88	70,634.80	77,366.55	84,905.96	93,356.61	102,848.51	113,510.12
23	4,197.50	349.79	11.50	50,370.00	54,808.39	59,771.48	65,330.52	71,566.96	78,573.91	86,457.99	95,340.71	105,361.68	116,680.15	129,478.39
24	4,380.00	365.00	12.00	54,750.00	59,780.27	65,434.51	71,801.84	78,984.83	87,101.61	96,288.16	106,701.15	118,521.01	131,955.56	147,244.22
25	4,562.50	380.21	12.50	59,312.50	64,989.21	71,396.95	78,655.27	86,889.23	96,247.31	106,901.70	119,052.11	132,930.19	148,804.69	166,987.39
26	4,745.00	395.42	13.00	64,057.50	70,428.51	77,664.79	85,902.28	95,299.60	106,041.93	118,345.51	132,462.91	148,089.21	167,369.10	188,905.63
27	4,927.50	410.63	13.50	68,985.00	76,109.97	84,244.14	93,554.67	104,236.18	116,517.90	130,669.39	147,007.74	165,906.04	187,803.36	213,216.45
28	5,110.00	425.83	14.00	74,095.00	82,031.77	91,141.22	101,624.61	113,720.03	127,709.29	143,926.15	162,765.98	184,697.33	210,275.56	240,159.09
29	5,292.50	441.04	14.50	79,387.50	88,197.51	98,362.40	110,124.63	123,773.03	139,651.88	158,171.77	179,822.57	205,189.01	234,969.19	269,996.75
30	5,475.00	456.25	15.00	84,862.50	94,609.24	105,914.15	119,067.61	134,417.95	152,388.23	173,465.57	198,268.40	227,517.13	262,084.17	303,018.93
31	5,657.50	471.46	15.50	90,520.00	101,269.41	113,803.08	128,466.87	145,678.47	165,942.76	189,870.46	218,200.72	251,828.60	291,838.42	339,544.07
32	5,840.00	486.67	16.00	96,360.00	108,180.50	122,035.94	138,336.07	157,579.21	180,371.90	207,453.09	239,723.57	278,282.09	324,469.47	379,922.47
33	6,022.50	501.88	16.50	102,382.50	115,345.03	130,619.61	148,689.33	170,145.78	195,714.12	226,284.12	262,948.29	307,048.96	360,236.25	424,539.47
34	6,205.00	517.08	17.00	108,587.50	122,765.53	139,561.10	159,541.16	183,404.81	212,015.08	246,438.47	287,994.02	338,314.28	399,420.97	473,818.92
35	6,387.50	532.29	17.50	114,975.00	130,444.56	148,867.57	170,906.52	197,384.00	229,322.71	267,995.53	314,988.23	372,277.92	442,331.29	528,227.06
36	6,570.00	547.50	18.00	121,545.00	138,384.71	158,546.32	182,800.82	212,112.16	247,687.34	291,039.46	344,067.30	409,155.75	489,302.34	588,276.77
37	6,752.50	562.71	18.50	128,297.50	146,588.58	168,604.80	195,239.92	227,619.25	267,161.83	315,694.48	375,377.19	449,180.91	540,699.77	654,532.19
38	6,935.00	577.92	19.00	135,232.50	155,058.81	179,050.60	208,240.16	243,936.42	287,801.68	341,950.15	409,074.04	492,605.18	596,921.90	727,613.91
39	7,117.50	593.13	19.50	142,350.00	163,798.08	189,891.46	221,818.39	261,096.07	309,665.13	370,011.70	445,324.65	539,700.50	658,402.95	808,204.56
40	7,300.00	608.33	20.00	149,650.00	172,800.06	201,135.29	235,991.95	279,131.91	332,813.89	399,950.41	484,308.70	590,760.54	725,616.21	897,055.01
41	7,482.50	623.54	20.50	157,132.50	182,094.47	212,790.14	250,778.68	298,078.99	357,310.69	431,878.88	526,216.58	646,102.48	799,077.60	994,991.26
42	7,665.00	638.75	21.00	164,797.50	191,657.07	224,864.25	266,196.99	317,973.75	383,224.47	465,916.51	571,253.29	706,068.83	879,349.43	1,102,921.89
43	7,847.50	653.96	21.50	172,645.00	201,499.61	237,365.98	282,265.82	338,854.10	410,625.57	502,189.85	610,687.85	771,029.69	967,044.66	1,221,846.33
44	8,030.00	669.17	22.00	180,675.00	211,624.91	250,308.90	299,004.70	360,754.97	439,588.35	540,833.05	671,604.60	841,384.46	1,062,881.38	1,352,863.96
45	8,212.50	684.38	22.50	188,887.50	222,035.78	263,686.73	316,433.71	383,730.84	470,190.89	581,988.28	727,404.29	917,564.72	1,167,437.82	1,497,184.11
46	8,395.00	699.58	23.00	197,282.50	232,735.09	277,523.36	334,573.58	407,810.88	502,515.18	625,806.28	787,305.24	1,000,036.50	1,281,656.67	1,656,137.02
47	8,577.50	714.79	23.50	205,860.00	243,725.72	291,822.88	353,445.61	433,043.91	536,647.32	672,446.80	851,594.53	1,089,303.12	1,406,256.45	1,831,185.97
48	8,760.00	730.00	24.00	214,620.00	255,010.57	306,594.54	373,071.78	459,476.07	572,677.68	722,079.21	920,579.35	1,185,908.17	1,542,476.93	2,023,940.57
49	8,942.50	745.21	24.50	223,562.50	266,592.61	321,847.78	393,474.70	487,155.31	610,701.19	774,883.01	994,588.38	1,290,438.72	1,691,047.18	2,236,171.37
50	9,125.00	760.42	25.00	232,687.50	278,474.78	337,592.23	414,677.70	516,131.52	650,716.50	831,048.49	1,073,973.32	1,403,528.82	1,853,528.87	2,469,826.01
51	9,307.50	775.63	25.50	241,995.00	290,660.10	353,837.73	436,704.75	546,456.59	693,131.25	890,777.35	1,159,110.48	1,525,963.23	2,030,119.75	2,727,046.86
52	9,490.00	790.83	26.00	251,485.00	303,151.61	370,594.28	459,580.59	578,164.45	737,752.32	954,289.19	1,250,402.51	1,658,181.48	2,223,803.36	3,010,190.55
53	9,672.50	806.04	26.50	261,157.50	315,952.35	387,872.12	483,330.69	611,371.23	784,796.06	1,021,793.25	1,348,280.26	1,801,282.30	2,433,803.36	3,321,849.35
54	9,855.00	821.25	27.00	271,012.50	329,065.42	405,681.66	507,981.26	646,075.28	834,383.61	1,093,547.14	1,453,204.73	1,956,028.20	2,663,582.62	3,664,874.79
55	10,037.50	836.46	27.50	281,050.00	342,493.95	424,033.55	533,559.32	682,873.27	886,642.17	1,169,799.72	1,565,469.18	2,123,351.05	2,914,251.38	4,042,403.51
56	10,220.00	851.67	28.00	291,270.00	356,241.09	442,938.62	560,092.70	720,280.38	941,705.27	1,250,820.90	1,686,201.43	2,304,256.73	3,187,673.80	4,457,885.86
57	10,402.50	866.88	28.50	301,672.50	370,310.02	462,407.94	587,610.06	759,010.19	999,713.70	1,338,896.81	1,815,366.20	2,499,831.97	3,485,903.17	4,915,117.20
58	10,585.00	882.08	29.00	312,257.50	384,709.97	482,452.80	616,140.91	801,315.00	1,060,813.07	1,428,330.72	1,953,767.79	2,711,250.33	3,811,172.10	5,418,272.42
59	10,767.50	897.29	29.50	323,025.00	399,426.19	503,084.70	645,715.66	844,565.80	1,125,158.60	1,525,444.11	2,102,052.76	2,939,779.26	4,165,914.17	5,971,943.91
60	10,950.00	912.50	30.00	333,975.00	414,479.05	524,315.40	676,365.63	889,736.43	1,192,915.08	1,628,577.78	2,260,912.95	3,186,787.60	4,552,781.94	6,581,183.31
61	11,132.50	927.71	30.50	345,107.50	429,868.58	546,156.86	708,123.07	936,903.66	1,264,249.96	1,738,092.87	2,431,084.63	3,453,753.71	4,974,666.74	7,251,547.39
62	11,315.00	942.92	31.00	356,422.50	445,595.41	568,621.29	741,021.22	986,147.44	1,339,343.21	1,854,372.34	2,613,371.88	3,742,274.20	5,434,720.10	7,989,148.62
63	11,497.50	958.13	31.50	367,920.00	461,663.84	591,721.17	775,044.28	1,037,550.74	1,418,382.74	1,977,822.03	2,808,610.24	4,054,073.44	5,936,377.18	8,800,710.74
64	11,680.00	973.33	32.00	379,600.00	478,077.28	615,469.19	810,377.51	1,091,199.97	1,501,565.88	2,108,872.16	3,017,710.56	4,391,013.71	6,483,382.33	9,693,629.81
65	11,862.50	988.54	32.50	391,462.50	494,839.18	639,878.33	846,907.21	1,147,184.96	1,589,099.80	2,247,978.74	3,241,643.17	4,755,106.31	7,079,816.86	10,676,041.54
66	12,045.00	1,003.75	33.00	403,507.50	511,953.02	664,961.79	884,720.77	1,205,599.16	1,681,202.04	2,395,625.16	3,481,446.34	5,148,523.42	7,730,129.43	11,756,895.20
67	12,227.50	1,018.96	33.50	415,735.00	529,422.33	690,733.08	923,856.72	1,266,539.73	1,778,011.01	2,552,323.82	3,738,231.01	5,573,610.90	8,439,169.06	12,946,084.97
68	12,410.00	1,034.17	34.00	428,145.00	547,250.65	717,205.94	964,354.72	1,330,107.72	1,880,036.56	2,718,617.85	4,018,185.68	6,032,902.67	9,212,321.17	14,254,289.46
69	12,592.50	1,049.38	34.50	440,737.50	565,441.58	744,394.41	1,006,255.64	1,396,408.23	1,987,280.52	2,894,860.14	4,307,582.87	6,529,134.78	10,055,046.90	15,693,570.16
70	12,775.00	1,064.58	35.00	453,512.50	583,998.74	772,312.80	1,049,601.56	1,465,550.56	2,100,037.29	3,082,329.45	4,622,782.92	7,065,262.56	10,973,925.87	17,276,979.67
71	12,957.50	1,079.79	35.50	466,470.00	602,925.81	800,975.70	1,094,435.83	1,537,648.38	2,218,644.53	3,281,004.17	4,960,242.25	7,644,477.67	11,970,787.37	19,018,930.89
72	13,140.00	1,095.00	36.00	479,610.00	622,236.47	830,398.02	1,140,803.10	1,612,819.91	2,343,373.76	3,491,782.82	5,321,519.01	8,270,227.08	13,067,838.73	20,985,277.98
73	13,322.50	1,110.21	36.50	492,932.50	641,939.18	860,594.93	1,188,183.12	1,691,188.11	2,474,531.07	3,715,422.23	5,708,422.85	8,946,233.55	14,258,460.54	23,043,460.53
74	13,505.00	1,125.42	37.00	506,437.50	661,963.55	891,581.92	1,238,322.00	1,772,880.83	2,612,437.88	3,952,662.87	6,122,310.39	9,676,517.63	15,556,448.11	25,362,062.08
75	13,687.50	1,140.63	37.50	520,125.00	682,407.56	923,374.81	1,289,569.79	1,858,031.07	2,757,431.64	4,204,331.39	6,565,517.74	10,465,421.54	16,971,447.82	27,913,084.54

10 cents a day times age

Age	Annual (US$)	Monthly (US$)	Daily (US$)	Total Investment (US$)	Compounding +1%	Compounding +2%	Compounding +3%	Compounding +4%	Compounding +5%	Compounding +6%	Compounding +7%	Compounding +8%	Compounding +9%	Compounding +10%
1	36.50	3.04	0.10	36.50	36.87	37.23	37.60	37.96	38.33	38.69	39.06	39.42	39.79	40.15
2	73.00	6.08	0.20	109.50	110.96	112.43	113.91	115.40	116.89	118.39	119.90	121.41	122.94	124.47
3	109.50	9.13	0.30	219.00	222.67	226.37	230.12	233.89	237.71	241.56	245.46	249.39	253.35	257.36
4	146.00	12.17	0.40	365.00	372.35	379.82	387.40	395.09	402.90	410.82	418.86	427.02	435.30	443.70
5	182.50	15.21	0.50	547.50	560.40	573.57	587.00	600.69	614.67	628.92	643.45	658.28	673.40	688.82
6	219.00	18.25	0.60	766.50	787.20	808.42	830.18	852.48	875.35	898.79	922.83	947.46	972.71	998.60
7	255.50	21.29	0.70	1,022.00	1,053.12	1,085.20	1,118.25	1,152.30	1,187.39	1,223.55	1,260.81	1,299.20	1,338.75	1,379.51
8	292.00	24.33	0.80	1,314.00	1,358.58	1,404.74	1,452.55	1,502.07	1,553.36	1,606.48	1,661.51	1,718.49	1,777.52	1,838.66
9	328.50	27.38	0.90	1,642.50	1,703.95	1,767.91	1,834.48	1,903.80	1,975.95	2,051.08	2,129.31	2,210.75	2,295.56	2,383.89
10	365.00	30.42	1.00	2,007.50	2,089.64	2,175.56	2,265.47	2,359.55	2,458.00	2,561.05	2,668.91	2,781.81	2,900.01	3,023.76
11	401.50	33.46	1.10	2,409.00	2,516.05	2,628.61	2,746.98	2,871.49	3,002.48	3,140.30	3,285.34	3,437.98	3,598.65	3,767.79
12	438.00	36.50	1.20	2,847.00	2,983.59	3,127.94	3,280.53	3,441.87	3,612.50	3,793.00	3,983.97	4,186.06	4,399.95	4,626.37
13	474.50	39.54	1.30	3,321.50	3,492.67	3,674.49	3,867.68	4,073.02	4,291.35	4,523.55	4,770.56	5,033.40	5,313.15	5,610.96
14	511.00	42.58	1.40	3,832.50	4,043.71	4,269.20	4,510.04	4,767.38	5,042.47	5,336.62	5,651.27	5,987.95	6,348.32	6,734.15
15	547.50	45.63	1.50	4,380.00	4,637.12	4,913.03	5,209.27	5,527.48	5,869.47	6,237.17	6,632.68	7,058.29	7,516.45	8,009.82
16	584.00	48.67	1.60	4,964.00	5,273.33	5,606.97	5,967.06	6,355.94	6,776.14	7,230.44	7,721.85	8,253.67	8,829.49	9,453.20
17	620.50	51.71	1.70	5,584.50	5,952.77	6,352.02	6,785.19	7,255.50	7,766.47	8,321.99	8,926.32	9,584.11	10,300.49	11,081.07
18	657.00	54.75	1.80	6,241.50	6,675.86	7,149.20	7,665.46	8,229.00	8,844.65	9,517.73	10,254.15	11,060.40	11,943.66	12,911.87
19	693.50	57.79	1.90	6,935.00	7,443.06	7,999.55	8,609.72	9,279.40	10,015.05	10,823.91	11,713.99	12,694.21	13,774.50	14,965.91
20	730.00	60.83	2.00	7,665.00	8,254.79	8,904.14	9,619.92	10,409.77	11,282.31	12,247.14	13,315.06	14,498.14	15,809.91	17,265.50
21	766.50	63.88	2.10	8,431.50	9,111.50	9,864.06	10,698.01	11,623.32	12,651.25	13,794.46	15,067.21	16,485.82	18,068.29	19,835.20
22	803.00	66.92	2.20	9,234.50	10,013.65	10,880.40	11,846.04	12,923.38	14,126.96	15,473.31	16,981.19	18,671.92	20,569.70	22,702.02
23	839.50	69.96	2.30	10,074.00	10,961.68	11,954.30	13,066.10	14,313.39	15,714.78	17,291.58	19,068.14	21,072.34	23,336.03	25,895.68
24	876.00	73.00	2.40	10,950.00	11,956.05	13,086.90	14,360.37	15,796.97	17,420.32	19,257.63	21,340.23	23,704.20	26,391.11	29,448.84
25	912.50	76.04	2.50	11,862.50	12,997.24	14,279.39	15,731.05	17,377.85	19,249.46	21,380.34	23,810.42	26,586.04	29,760.94	33,397.48
26	949.00	79.08	2.60	12,811.50	14,085.70	15,532.06	17,180.46	19,059.92	21,208.39	23,669.10	26,492.58	29,737.84	33,473.83	37,781.13
27	985.50	82.13	2.70	13,797.00	15,221.91	16,848.83	18,710.93	20,847.24	23,303.58	26,133.88	29,401.55	33,181.21	37,560.67	42,643.29
28	1,022.00	85.17	2.80	14,819.00	16,406.35	18,228.24	20,324.92	22,744.01	25,541.86	28,785.23	32,553.20	36,939.47	42,055.11	48,031.80
29	1,058.50	88.21	2.90	15,877.50	17,639.50	19,672.48	22,024.93	24,754.61	27,930.38	31,634.35	35,964.51	41,037.80	46,993.84	53,999.35
30	1,095.00	91.25	3.00	16,972.50	18,921.85	21,182.83	23,813.52	26,883.59	30,476.65	34,693.11	39,653.68	45,503.43	52,416.83	60,603.79
31	1,131.50	94.29	3.10	18,104.00	20,253.88	22,760.62	25,693.37	29,135.69	33,188.55	37,974.09	43,640.14	50,365.72	58,367.68	67,908.81
32	1,168.00	97.33	3.20	19,272.00	21,636.10	24,407.19	27,667.21	31,515.84	36,074.38	41,490.62	47,944.71	55,656.42	64,893.89	75,984.49
33	1,204.50	100.38	3.30	20,476.50	23,069.01	26,123.92	29,737.87	34,029.16	39,142.82	45,256.82	52,589.66	61,409.79	72,047.25	84,907.89
34	1,241.00	103.42	3.40	21,717.50	24,553.11	27,912.22	31,908.23	36,680.96	42,408.02	49,287.69	57,598.80	67,662.86	79,884.19	94,763.78
35	1,277.50	106.46	3.50	22,995.00	26,088.91	29,773.51	34,181.30	39,476.85	45,864.54	53,599.11	62,997.65	74,455.58	88,466.25	105,645.41
36	1,314.00	109.50	3.60	24,309.00	27,676.94	31,709.26	36,560.16	42,422.43	49,537.47	58,207.89	68,813.46	81,813.15	97,860.47	117,655.35
37	1,350.50	112.54	3.70	25,659.00	29,317.72	33,720.96	39,047.98	45,523.85	53,432.37	63,131.90	75,075.44	89,836.18	108,139.95	130,906.44
38	1,387.00	115.58	3.80	27,046.50	31,011.76	35,810.12	41,648.03	48,787.28	57,560.34	68,390.03	81,814.81	98,521.04	119,384.38	145,512.86
39	1,423.50	118.63	3.90	28,470.00	32,759.62	37,978.29	44,363.68	52,219.21	61,933.03	74,002.34	89,064.99	107,940.10	131,680.59	161,640.91
40	1,460.00	121.67	4.00	29,930.00	34,561.81	40,227.06	47,198.39	55,826.38	66,562.68	79,990.08	96,861.74	118,152.11	145,123.24	179,411.00
41	1,496.50	124.71	4.10	31,426.50	36,418.89	42,558.03	50,155.74	59,615.80	71,462.14	86,375.78	105,243.32	129,220.50	159,815.52	198,998.25
42	1,533.00	127.75	4.20	32,959.50	38,331.41	44,972.85	53,239.40	63,594.75	76,644.89	93,183.30	114,213.78	141,213.78	175,869.89	220,584.38
43	1,569.50	130.79	4.30	34,529.00	40,299.92	47,473.20	56,453.16	67,770.82	82,125.11	100,437.97	123,927.57	154,205.94	193,408.93	244,369.27
44	1,606.00	133.83	4.40	36,135.00	42,324.98	50,060.78	59,800.94	72,151.89	87,917.67	108,166.61	134,320.92	168,276.80	212,566.28	270,512.79
45	1,642.50	136.88	4.50	37,777.50	44,407.16	52,737.35	63,286.74	76,746.17	94,038.18	116,397.66	145,480.86	183,512.94	233,487.56	299,436.82
46	1,679.00	139.92	4.60	39,456.50	46,547.02	55,504.67	66,914.72	81,562.18	100,503.04	125,161.26	157,461.05	200,007.30	256,331.56	331,227.40
47	1,715.50	142.96	4.70	41,172.00	48,745.14	58,364.58	70,689.12	86,608.78	107,329.46	134,489.36	170,318.91	217,860.62	281,271.29	366,237.19
48	1,752.00	146.00	4.80	42,924.00	51,002.11	61,318.91	74,614.36	91,895.21	114,535.54	144,415.84	184,115.07	237,181.63	308,495.39	404,784.12
49	1,788.50	149.04	4.90	44,712.50	53,318.52	64,369.56	78,694.94	97,431.06	122,140.24	154,976.60	198,917.68	258,087.74	338,209.44	447,234.27
50	1,825.00	152.08	5.00	46,537.50	55,694.96	67,518.45	82,935.54	103,291.32	130,163.50	166,209.70	214,796.84	280,705.76	370,637.54	490,355.20
51	1,861.50	155.13	5.10	48,399.00	58,132.02	70,767.55	87,340.95	109,291.32	138,626.25	178,155.47	231,822.10	305,172.65	406,023.95	545,409.37
52	1,898.00	158.17	5.20	50,297.00	60,630.32	74,118.86	91,916.12	115,636.89	147,550.46	190,856.68	250,063.50	331,636.30	444,634.92	602,038.11
53	1,934.50	161.21	5.30	52,231.50	63,190.47	77,574.42	96,666.14	122,274.25	156,059.21	204,358.65	269,656.05	360,256.46	486,760.67	664,369.87
54	1,971.00	164.25	5.40	54,202.50	65,813.08	81,136.33	101,596.25	129,215.06	166,876.72	218,709.43	290,640.95	391,205.66	532,717.52	732,974.96
55	2,007.50	167.29	5.50	56,210.00	68,498.79	84,806.71	106,711.86	136,471.46	177,328.43	233,959.84	313,133.84	424,670.21	582,850.28	808,480.70
56	2,044.00	170.33	5.60	58,254.00	71,248.22	88,587.72	112,018.54	144,056.08	188,341.05	250,164.18	337,240.29	460,851.35	637,534.76	891,577.17
57	2,080.50	173.38	5.70	60,334.50	74,062.00	92,481.59	117,522.01	151,982.04	199,942.63	267,379.36	363,073.24	499,066.39	697,180.63	983,023.44
58	2,117.00	176.42	5.80	62,451.50	76,940.79	96,490.58	123,228.18	160,263.00	212,162.61	285,666.14	390,753.56	542,250.07	762,234.42	1,083,654.48
59	2,153.50	179.46	5.90	64,605.00	79,885.24	100,616.94	129,143.13	168,913.16	225,031.92	305,088.82	420,410.55	587,955.85	833,182.83	1,194,388.78
60	2,190.00	182.50	6.00	66,795.00	82,895.99	104,863.08	135,273.13	177,947.29	238,583.02	325,715.55	452,182.59	637,357.52	910,556.39	1,316,236.66
61	2,226.50	185.54	6.10	69,021.50	85,973.72	109,231.37	141,624.61	187,380.74	252,849.99	347,618.57	486,217.73	690,750.74	994,933.35	1,450,309.48
62	2,263.00	188.58	6.20	71,284.50	89,119.08	113,724.26	148,204.24	197,267.08	267,868.64	370,874.47	522,674.38	748,454.84	1,086,944.02	1,597,829.72
63	2,299.50	191.63	6.30	73,584.00	92,332.77	118,344.23	155,018.86	207,510.15	283,676.55	395,564.41	561,722.05	810,814.69	1,187,275.44	1,760,142.15
64	2,336.00	194.67	6.40	75,920.00	95,615.46	123,093.84	162,075.50	218,239.99	300,313.18	421,774.43	603,542.11	878,202.74	1,296,676.47	1,938,725.96
65	2,372.50	197.71	6.50	78,292.50	98,967.84	127,975.67	169,381.44	229,436.99	317,819.96	449,595.75	648,328.63	951,021.26	1,415,963.37	2,135,208.31
66	2,409.00	200.75	6.60	80,701.50	102,390.60	132,992.36	176,944.15	241,119.83	336,240.41	479,125.03	696,358.56	1,029,704.08	1,546,025.89	2,351,379.04
67	2,445.50	203.79	6.70	83,147.00	105,884.46	138,146.62	184,771.34	253,307.95	355,620.20	510,464.76	747,646.20	1,114,722.20	1,687,833.81	2,589,206.99
68	2,482.00	206.83	6.80	85,629.00	109,450.13	143,441.19	192,870.94	266,021.54	376,007.31	543,723.57	802,637.18	1,206,580.53	1,842,444.23	2,850,857.89
69	2,518.50	209.88	6.90	88,147.50	113,088.32	148,878.88	201,251.13	279,281.65	397,452.10	579,016.59	861,516.57	1,305,826.96	2,011,009.38	3,138,714.03
70	2,555.00	212.92	7.00	90,702.50	116,799.75	154,462.56	209,920.31	293,081.40	420,007.46	616,465.89	924,546.58	1,413,052.51	2,194,785.17	3,455,905.93
71	2,591.50	215.96	7.10	93,294.00	120,585.16	160,195.14	218,887.17	307,529.68	443,728.91	656,200.83	992,048.45	1,528,895.53	2,395,140.57	3,803,786.18
72	2,628.00	219.00	7.20	95,922.00	124,445.29	166,079.60	228,160.62	322,560.52	468,550.49	698,358.56	1,064,303.80	1,654,045.42	2,613,567.75	4,187,055.60
73	2,664.50	222.04	7.30	98,586.50	128,380.89	172,118.99	237,749.87	338,237.62	494,906.21	743,084.45	1,141,656.08	1,789,246.71	2,851,693.15	4,608,692.11
74	2,701.00	225.08	7.40	101,287.50	132,392.71	178,316.38	247,644.40	354,576.17	522,487.58	790,532.57	1,224,462.08	1,935,303.53	3,111,289.62	5,072,532.42
75	2,737.50	228.13	7.50	104,025.00	136,481.51	184,674.96	257,913.96	371,606.21	551,486.33	840,866.28	1,313,103.55	2,093,084.31	3,394,289.56	5,582,796.91

I've heard some say they were reluctant to invest in the stock market because they see it as similar to 'gambling'.

If you have the same concern, consider investing in the stock market as a 'partnership' (not gambling) with a company / fund, where you are becoming a fractional owner of a company / fund to which you have done research, entrusting them to make your share grow.

With everything mentioned above, after studying to understand the risks and opportunities that come with investing, you will realize that, over time, the opportunities for growth greatly outweighs the risks involved.

In order to increase the potential and speed of growth in your wealth, investing in the stock market (to join the partnership with companies / funds), is one of the best ways to help your financial 'dust' grow, until it becomes a 'mountain' that you can call "Financial Freedom".

CHAPTER 5: QUALITY MINDSET

In the final three chapters, I would like to share additional ideas and mindset that has helped me to improve and succeed throughout my career.

Each idea and mindset described will indirectly support the progress toward financial success.

As with financial mindset, quality mindset builds with time and exposure to various experiences.

Below is my philosophy at the workplace, which also summarizes the way I think in general, and how I approach everything in life.

Reading through these chapters, connecting from the beginning to the end, I hope you will see that the overall mindset you develop through time and effort, becomes greater than the sum of all parts.

In any team-oriented environment, **Quality comes from the mindset** of each individual within the entire team (whether it be with co-workers, or with family and friends).

How to achieve and maintain High Level Quality (7 pointers to remember at all times):

1) Do everything as if you were the receiver of everything you do.

2) Maintain willingness to comprehend and follow the requirements (work instructions / standards / specifications / procedures).

3) Listen / Respect / Strive to understand.

4) Don't assume anything / Ask questions.

5) Share the knowledge / information.

6) Keep an open mind / Don't criticize before attempting to understand.

7) Focus on your own responsibilities first; realize that you cannot control what others do; there is no way for you to know all that others go through (only after you complete / master your responsibilities, can you attempt to help / guide others).

"Skill" / "Development" does not always come from the number of years you spend in the field, no matter what your profession, and no matter where you come from; it comes from the mindset -- how well you interpret, understand, soak in the experience, and how well you practice the 7 pointers listed above.

Quality in various aspects of life (professional or personal) is a result of the accumulation of appreciation, respect, and pride.

Appreciate the opportunities you are given, respect everything and everyone around you, remain proud of all of your daily efforts/ accomplishments, and quality will naturally follow.

Quality = Appreciation + Respect + Pride

CHAPTER 6: IDEAS AT WORK

Below are 18 observations compiled based on various interactions at work (in no particular order), which I believe will help certain personalities to reflect on themselves, as reminders for continued self- improvement.

Whether it be addressing themselves, or to better understand others with certain tendencies, to potentially help guide others to also improve.

Take one or two items a day (don't take in all at once).

Try to identify and address / improve negative 'dust' as soon as possible, so it does not become a 'mountain' of negatives that may drag you down.

And focus on building various positive 'mountains'.

Again, ideas at the workplace often applies to life in general.

1) Put your ego aside, and listen with an open mind, always with intent to support, whether it be to agree with what others say, or to support by directing them to a better path (sometimes this is difficult when the person you are talking to tends to be close minded or incompetent at the time, but be patient with intent to support).

2) Be open to various questions, as many questions raised may be used to verify and clarify topics to minimize potential for confusion.

And be open to take in ideas outside of own thinking, as long as the idea comes with full understanding of the process and product in discussion, with consideration of the initial intent of the process before the idea is proposed or implemented.

And evaluate whether or not the idea being proposed is logically practical and value added.

3) Be sure to verify your own work before presenting to others.

If you present incorrect information, be sure to follow-up to clarify any confusion, as any concern and action that came about prior to the correction may be wasted effort.

4) Think carefully about what others are saying, and keep in mind there is always a possibility you are initially incorrect in interpretation, or simply misunderstanding.

If you confirm that the other side is incorrectly interpreting or misunderstanding the topic being discussed, do not be judgmental, and kindly support them until they have a good understanding.

5) Be able to constructively debate with full understanding of the process and product, by first considering the facts and data / information to support your perspective.

Avoid argument, unless it can be confirmed that a claim or criticism is definitely coming from lack of understanding of the topic being discussed.

6) If more than 2 people have told you that you should listen and/or change the way you think on separate occasions, realize that there is most likely something you need to change.

Take a step back and evaluate if you are the common denominator to various communication struggles, and refine your approach.

7) If you are going to complain about getting reprimanded for delaying or neglecting something, just get it done correctly and timely before that happens (acknowledge that you are the cause of your own frustration).

8) Being a practical thinker does not mean taking shortcuts.

Being practical is to find realistic ways to be efficient and effective in achieving what ultimately needs to be accomplished, through actionable steps, while maintaining the original purpose / intent with rational / logical thinking, and knowing enough about the process, product, and purpose.

9) It is important to understand and follow existing rules, but simply to 'go by the book' without considering all possible options to achieve the same goal, is not always the best path.

It is easy to 'go by the book' (where this becomes the only option for those who do not have full understanding of a given process), but to continue improving and to grow, one must strive to be able to evaluate various options to become logically practical, while always considering all of the potential risks involved.

10) Don't get influenced by those that tend to speak in hindsight, or criticize someone or something after the fact, without being able to directly address potential concerns before issues occur, or without having any backbone to their statements.

They are the ones that tend to speak behind others' backs, to always look for distractions to cover their lack of understanding or insecurities.

Instead, listen to those comments, focus on developing your own knowledge and skills to be able to support yourself and the tasks at hand, and look for ways to lead / support the team to think and move forward, always with a positive / forward thinking mindset.

11) Realize that others see through one's insecurities, and often feel some disappointment, whenever one speaks badly / negatively about someone else behind their backs.

Especially those in leadership roles must refrain from expressing negativity or disrespect about peers or subordinates behind their backs.

This only creates awkwardness and disappointment that a leader may also speak badly about the person listening, when they are not around.

Note: This is different from attempting to motivate by giving special credit / recognition to others, and different from attempting to make others realize actual negative influence.

12) There are those that complain no matter which way things go, as long as something requires them to be involved / responsible, and requires some action on their part.

To those personalities, it does not matter how well the communication is initiated.

The individual will complain that there was not enough information being shared at the time of their preference (they will resist or not cooperate because "information was not shared earlier"), and they will also complain when opportunity for communication is offered (they will not cooperate because they are "too busy for additional information").

No matter how careful others are to avoid making statements that may sound directed to that person, they will either take / interpret it personally (become defensive), or will make it sound like it was projected personally, as a form of defense to avoid having to take action / responsibility themselves.

13) There is no reason to compare your experience / workload / work ethic with others, because it will be comparing totally different things through assumptions, and the comparison will usually be inaccurate (there is no way to know exactly what others are tasked to do, or to know everything they are going through).

Even if someone tends to appear not so busy, they may simply be capable of completing their tasks more efficiently than the one who is complaining that they are "too busy" all of the time, or others may be able to complete similar tasks while making it look easy.

Whatever the case, focus on your own tasks / responsibilities, and become self-motivated about what you can do (rather than being focused on 'what others should do'; unless you are tasked to manage others).

14) It's mostly in the way you think.

Unless you have the self-motivated initiative, and the drive to learn and improve yourself, you will risk being dissatisfied, no matter where you go or what you do.

If you ever feel like your current position / situation is dissatisfying, whether at work or in your personal life, first take the effort to list out what you can do to make the situation closer to what you consider your ideal.

Make sure to list what **you** can do, and not what you expect others to do, because you cannot control what others do, but you have full control of what you can do (take full responsibility to change what you consider dissatisfying).

Sometimes, all it takes is to adjust the way you think about the situation.

15) Always consider how to help yourself be and feel 'better', by interpreting everything with flexibility (with a grain of salt, benefit of the doubt, etc.), and consider what will result in a positive outcome for yourself, while maintaining respect to others in any situation.

Whenever you have problems communicating or interacting with a certain individual, in order to avoid getting frustrated / angry / stressed / offended / etc. about the situation, help yourself by considering that the reason for the difficulty may be because the certain individual is simply having a bad day, or there may be something you need to change in the approach to make the situation better.

In order to avoid becoming frustrated / angry / stressed / offended / etc., always consider how to take any interaction in any situation to your advantage (figuratively speaking), by looking for the positives in everything.

Before you take offense to anything, help yourself by considering that your interpretation / assumption to what others are implying may be incorrect.

Think of how you can help make the situation better, with an open mind, respect, and understanding, where you can keep positive by being proud of being a better person to be able to help others through your positive approach.

Even in situations where a person may actually be intending to offend you, by taking the above approach, you will always be helping yourself feel better about the situation, knowing you are attempting to be helpful (to yourself first, and then to others) in any given situation.

If all else fails to make the situation better, step aside to organize your thoughts, consult someone you can rely on for support, and consider whether or not the situation is worth reapproaching.

16) Provide employees training on self-motivation, leadership, team building and multidisciplinary approach, so they can better understand the concept of leading teams and holding team meetings themselves.

Let them know up front, that the training is for them to be better capable of providing constructive feedback and ideas during various meetings and projects that others lead, rather than simply complaining or criticizing about what or how 'others' are doing.

By learning what a leader goes through, they can also learn to be respectful and involved when others are leading, to be open and self-motivated to develop ideas for improvement with a team oriented mindset, and to be able to guide themselves to gain benefits from various meetings and projects.

After the training, ask them to always look for ways to help make meetings and projects efficient and effective by supporting all participants involved.

17) What every for-profit business and paid employee needs to constantly remind themselves:

1) The basic difference between them and the customer: they are getting paid to provide customer service / courtesy, which is what customers are paying for.

2) Without paying customers, their business / job will not exist.

3) They chose to be in the business / job; the customer did not ask them to be doing what they are getting paid to do (to provide customer service).

4) If they are unwilling to provide customer service, they should look for another profession. Nobody is asking or forcing them to do what they are getting paid to do.

5) If they do not want to hear customer complaints, do their job professionally before anyone tells them to. That is what they are getting paid to do.

6) Do everything as if they were the receiver of everything they do.

18) What every customer requesting service needs to constantly remind themselves:

1) Service providers are there to help / support them.

2) Without service providers, they will have to complete the task themselves.

3) Both they (paying to have task completed) and the service provider (getting paid to complete task) rely on each other.

4) They pay for the service, and service provider gives them service for the payment; it's an equal give-and-take (as long as the service provider follows item 17 above).

5) Both they and the service provider deserve mutual respect.

Denial is one of the worst things to keep you from becoming a dependable / reliable person.

Maintaining the willingness to listen to others, and attempting to always understand others' perspectives, are the keys to open-mindedness and continuous improvement.

It is important to know the traits of people that have reliable personalities, to strive to become one, but just as important is to know the traits of people that are considered to have unreliable personalities, so that you know what not to be, and who to help.

Each positive or negative habit accumulates, to build up to your overall personality, and ultimately to your success or failure.

Gather as much of the positives as you can, to let them grow in any situation, and continue to minimize and manage the negatives.

CHAPTER 7: RELIABLE / UNRELIABLE PERSONALITIES

Do you see yourself as a reliable figure to society (to family, friends, workplace, community, etc.)?

Do you think others consider you to be dependable / reliable?

Do you see yourself more toward being somewhat unreliable?

Do you sometimes feel that you may not be creating added value to your surroundings?

Do you consider or even care how others see you, whether you influence others positively or negatively?

Being considered dependable / reliable often comes from proven track record and reputation that develop over time.

However, time and experience could become less meaningful unless you maintain a positive mindset, to be open and keep the willingness to continue to improve.

Even if someone has 30 years of experience at something, if they have been doing it inefficiently or incorrectly for most of the 30 years, with a closed mind, they will add less value or even negative value, compared to a newer person who strives to learn the best practices and continues to look for opportunities to improve with an open mind.

It's not always about experience, degree, or certification.

It's mostly about the mindset.

I believe people that are considered dependable / reliable demonstrate the following traits (20 in no particular order):

If you have these traits, keep at it, and continue to improve.

If you currently do not have these traits, practice, and strive to improve.

1) Keeps an open mind.

2) Does not criticize before attempting to understand.

3) Always expects more from themselves than from others.

4) Does everything as if they are the receiver of everything they do.

5) Listens / Respects / Strives to understand.

6) Takes ownership of their own action and plan, rather than just talk.

7) Thinks carefully before taking action, and always verifies their work.

8) Shares knowledge and information.

9) Approaches everything with a supportive mind (listen / respond / act with intent to support).

10) Does not assume anything / Asks questions.

11) Maintains constant willingness to comprehend, and to follow requirements (instructions / standards / specifications / procedures).

12) Always remembers that it is easier said than done (understands that asking for something is easier than creating something).

13) Capable of adjusting as necessary if situation and facts change.

14) Observes and evaluates for themselves, rather than through second hand information.

15) Stays focused on their own responsibilities; realizes they cannot fully control what others do, and there is no way to know all that others are going through.

16) Understands that standards and baseline are important, but also that innovation and improvement often comes from flexibility.

17) Capable of completing tasks efficiently and effectively, by realizing priorities while keeping overall time management in mind.

18) Does not wait until tasks pile up; knows that the longer tasks are delayed, more tasks will build up, potentially creating more delays, and even inaccuracies.

19) Realizes that there are always more to learn.

20) Takes initiatives, to strive to continue improving on the items listed above.

Key Words for Reliable Personalities:

o   Open-minded / understanding

o   Respectful / thoughtful / kind

o   Considerate / careful

o   Curious (without being nosy)

o   Supportive

o   Detail oriented

o   Organized

o   Positive minded (thoughtfully optimistic)

o   Responsible (takes ownership of own actions)

o   Confident / decisive / assertive (not to be confused with arrogant)

o   Unassuming

o   Trusting

o   Unbiased

o   Rational / logical / practical thinking

o   Consistent

o   Honest / genuine

o   Uncalculating

o   Calm / gentle / relaxed

o   Patient

o   Motivated / active

o   Generous / giving

o   Humble

o   Selfless

o   Polite / courteous

o   Forgiving

o   Proactive / preventive

o   Prudent

o   Takes action / initiative without complaining

o   Good prioritization skills

o   Good time management

o   Continuous improvement

I believe people that are considered unreliable have the following traits (34 in no particular order):

If you have any of these traits, look for how you can improve and avoid.

If you encounter anyone else with these traits, support them to improve.

1) Will not read this column in full with an open mind, and will not attempt to see other's views to see if there is anything to take in for further self-improvement.

2) Lacks ability to fully listen, read, and comprehend.

3) Tends to think and speak in hindsight, and becomes quiet when important decisions are being made real-time.

4) Neglects the fact that their lack of communication skills, lack of actions, and lack of understanding, etc., often leads to issues they are complaining about.

5) Tells others to avoid "assumption" without understanding the difference between assumption and 'hypothesis', while not realizing that they are the ones that tend to assume that others are assuming.

6) Critical of everything with exception of themselves (often misunderstanding with skewed ideas on what they are criticizing).

7) Unable to complete tasks efficiently or effectively as they come, unable to realize priorities, with lack of overall time management.

8) Delays projects (small or large) until tasks pile up; does not realize that the longer tasks are put on hold, more tasks will build up on top of it, potentially creating more delays, and even inaccuracies.

9) Always blames others for their own lack of competency (waits for someone else to take action or to provide guidance, without taking initiatives).

10) Does not realize that if everyone always acted 'by the book', there will not be any innovation or continuous improvement.

11) Believes "explaining in ways that even a 3 year old will understand" literally applies to all audiences, and quite often becomes condescending / disrespectful.

12) Complains about being made to correct their inefficiencies resulting from their failure to communicate to fully understand, and fails to realize that taking time to do something correctly with full knowledge of expectations the first time, is much better than having to spend time correcting mistakes.

13) Asks random questions without full care for what is needed, and when an answer is received, only takes in pieces of the answer and somehow bends the conversation out of context.

14) Fails to fully see what others expect (lacks the care to fully listen and understand what others need).

15) Unable to improvise, adapt, or adjust based on current situation (always thinks the requirement is 'by the book', and is unwilling / unable to brainstorm potential for practical options and solutions while avoiding risks at the same time).

16) Uses generalized, vague examples and references, such as "in this industry" or "where I used to work", just so they do not have to show direct examples or proof of what they are stating, which may not actually exist.

17) Exaggerates concerns, to talk about 'how it should be' without being able to demonstrate 'how to get to where it should be'.

18) Always looks for excuses / cover-ups (example: always asks someone else to double-check their responsibility, just so they will not be fully responsible if something goes wrong)*.

*It is good to verify work/information with others, but if the act is simply to avoid being fully responsible for their own responsibilities, it only creates inefficiencies.

19) Tends to comment only on the obvious aspects of a topic in discussion, to appear correct (or simply agrees with someone that gives good ideas, even though they do not generate new ideas themselves), and avoids commenting on technical / important details in order to avoid being incorrect.

20) Acts busy in order to avoid the topic at hand, and always reserves an excuse, that they do not know because they were too busy at a particular time, or that someone did not notify them.

21) Jumps to conclusion without careful verfication of own theory, and without full consideration of any other logical ideas / possibilities / risks.

22) Rushes to implement "good ideas" without full understanding of the initial intent of the current process, potential risks, and other considerations (not realizing some ideas may be 'recreating the wheel' or increasing potential risks that others may have reviewed in the past to avoid).

23) Tends to focus on covering their insecurities or faults by placing all of the effort to appear confident, often without being able to demonstrate core knowledge (example: will not acknowledge their errors, and rather than trying to improve, places their effort in covering mistakes with random excuses).

24) Follows people that tend to talk and laugh about others behind their backs (without realizing that those people will likely also talk about them behind their back, and without fully understanding the overall situation themselves; unable to lead by setting good examples themselves).

25) Uses "nobody is perfect" as an excuse to not even attempt to improve, but criticize when others say the same.

26) Raises random concerns through misinterpretations, insecurities, and/or lack of knowledge regarding various topics in discussion.

Often raises concerns through their skewed mindset, assuming others will take similar approach as they think, such as making assumptions, taking shortcuts, not taking any actions, blaming others, denying own responsibility, or reacting in hindsight; all while not listening to what others say, even when those around them have a valid point.

And because of the above, they fail to see the overall picture and the practical solutions, in the meantime often creating unnecessary noise and impractical / illogical / ineffective / irrelevant workload to others.

27) Attempts to manipulate or bend the story, to cover and defend their insecurities or mistakes, and to avoid having to take action.

There are at least 2 types of manipulative personalities.

One that present positives on the surface but actually wishes and directs the negatives (example: says something to one group, but something opposite to another).

And another that bends / changes what they say or do mid-process as soon as they see something to their disadvantage, with disregard to potential impact to others (without acknowledging their mistake, or change in facts / situation).

Manipulative personalities either do not realize that their actions are obvious to others around them, or they simply do not have the capacity or integrity to care.

28) Builds false sense of confidence from their lack of experience to fail, not realizing that the lack of experience to fail is because they are not asked to lead or manage tasks due to their unreliability, and are not challenged, either to fail or to succeed.

29) Does not realize that the reason others tend to not bother to comment or to disagree with them, is because they are considered to hold no value in discussing the issue, due to their close-minded tendencies.

30) Indecisive and overly conservative (paranoid).

31) Reactive (not preventive).

32) Will not consider additional improvement or support when others are responsible.

33) Does not realize that there are always more to learn.

34) Will not take initiatives, to strive to continue improving on the items listed above.

Key Words for Unreliable Personalities:

o   Close-minded

o   Disrespectful / unthoughtful / unkind

o   Inconsiderate / Careless / rough

o   Unsupportive

o   Unorganized

o   Negative minded (overly pessimistic)

o   Irresponsible (always blaming others)

o   Insecure / indecisive / paranoid

o   All-assuming / know-it-all

o   Doubtful

o   Judgmental

o   Biased

o   Irrational / impractical

o   Inconsistent

o   Dishonest / deceptive / manipulative

o   Nervous / timid / tense

o   Demotivated / lazy

o   Stingy

o   Arrogant / egotistical

o   Selfish / self-centered

o   Jealous

o   Rude / condescending

o   Obnoxious

o   Unforgiving

o   Reactive

o   Complaining (without taking action themselves)

o   Lack prioritization skills

o   Lack time management skills

o   Complacent / Stagnant

I often think about which personality I fit into more often, reliable or unreliable, being completely honest with myself, and think about what the world would be like if everyone else had those personalities.

While realizing that 'nobody is perfect', and that I may occasionally show some unreliable personalities, I push myself to improve, to become a positive influence to everyone around me.

I try my best to avoid the unreliable personalities, and when I see myself tending towards any of them, I remind myself to do better.

I tell myself once again, to gather the positives, so that I can help to reduce the negatives.

I constantly remind myself, that the sooner I start anything with an open mind, the better things will be.

CLOSING

In summary, the concept of 'dust' accumulating to make a 'mountain' is universal.

If you consider your philosophy / mindset as a 'mountain', every idea / interpretation and experience you encounter are the 'dust' that accumulates to make that 'mountain'.

If you consider financial independence as a 'mountain', every savings and investments (Time / Energy / Money) are the 'dust' that accumulates to make that 'mountain'.

If you consider overall success (whatever it may be) as a 'mountain', everything you decide to pursue or address in between are the 'dust' that accumulates to make that 'mountain'.

Whether to grow a positive or a negative 'mountain', is always your choice.

With a positive mindset, and a clear target with a consistent investment strategy, I achieved my goal of financial independence, which now allows me to consider many more 'mountains' in my life.

Each individual operate in different ways, but I believe the mindset of many positively successful individuals must be similar in many ways.

If you want relief from financial stress, and relief from work related stress, please take this book as a message from a proof of concept, with an open mind.

Taking just some of these ideas should lead anyone toward a better path.

No matter what your goal may be, as long as you set a clear goal and take each step with the correct mindset in place, every one of us can make our positive 'dust' accumulate to become a 'mountain' of success.

APPENDIX
(Supplement to Financial Growth)

Aside from consistent investments leading to significant compounding growth, there are various ways to supplement the growth in wealth.

Using various points and cash back programs, and even retail coupons, I have saved thousands of dollars over several years, including free hotel stays and free flights, and hundreds of dollars in cash back each year.

Even seemingly insignificant amount could add up to be hundreds and thousands of dollars over several months and years, with very little extra effort.

And you could invest the additional money you save for even more compounding growth.

Credit Card

(As long as you commit yourself to pay off the entire statement amount each month)

- Points / Promotion

    o   Many credit cards offer sign-up bonus during promotional periods (points or cash bonus)

    o   Take advantage of various cash back or points credit card, which will add up to be hundreds / thousands of dollars over several years

    o   Close / cancel and rotate with other credit cards every 2 years or so, in order to take advantage of 2 year promotional reset (promotion usually applies only for new members or those that have been away from a particular card for over 2 year period)*

    *Keep one or two credit cards out of this rotation to maintain higher credit score (credit scores are impacted by the number of years you keep certain credits intact); as of this writing, I have maintained credit score above 800.

- Referral Bonus

  o Many credit cards also offer cash or points bonus for referring family and friends to open an account

  o Refer as many family and friends to sign-up to the credit card, up to max limit

  o Work with family and friends to close / cancel and rotate with other credit cards every 2 years or so, in order to take advantage of 2 year promotional and referral reset (promotion and referral bonus usually applies only for new members or those that have been away from a particular card for over 2 year period)*

  *Avoid doing this with family and friends if you are not confident that they will commit to maintaining good credit for themselves by paying off their entire statement amount each month (you do not want to create a potential burden for them).

- Examples of Credit Cards

Capital One Quicksilver
- o $200 sign-up bonus
- o 1.5% cash back for every purchase
- o $150 referral bonus
- o No Annual Fee

Chase IHG Rewards Club
- o Up to 160,000 points sign-up bonus
- o Platinum IHG Status
- o 1 Free Night Stay per year
- o Points for every purchase
- o 10,000 points referral bonus
- o $99 Annual Fee (After you receive the sign-up bonus, cancel prior to 1 year to avoid paying fee)

BofA Unlimited Cash Rewards
- o $200 sign-up bonus
- o Up to 50% cash back for various purchase
- o No Annual Fee

Various mileage cards

Free Points / Cash Back Program

Aside from the usual Hotel/Airline/ Rental Car points program, there are many cash back and points programs available for free.

- Rakuten (formerly Ebates)

- Ad site that gives unlimited cash back for everyday purchases online and in-store, just by going through their links (many major stores available)

- If you are going to shop anyway, might as well receive extra cash back (15% or more during promotions; in addition to credit card rewards and coupon discounts)

- $25+ referral bonus (www.rakuten.com/r/MATSUD12)

- Shopkick

- Ad site similar to Rakuten, where points are given to shoppers for everyday online and in-store purchase

- Unlike Rakuten, points can also be received just by walking into listed stores and opening the Shopkick app (no purchase required); you can often get points driving by with the app open

- Points can also be received by scanning barcodes of eligible items (no purchase required)

- Accumulated points are exchanged for a gift certificate to a store of your choice (Amazon, TJX, HomeDepot, Target, etc.)

- 250 points referral bonus (www.shopkick.com
Referral Code: DEAL329673)

- OpenTable
- Ad site that gives points for making and completing reservations
- Qualifying points may be exchanged for gift certificates to use in future reservations

- Coupon
- Old-school clipping coupons, or coupons through the store email or app
- $0.50, $1, 10%, 20%, BOGO, etc. over time grows to be hundreds of dollars saved
- Use coupons in addition to ad site points program like Rakuten or Shopkick, and the savings accumulate even more
- Every penny saved counts toward the first million dollars (whether it be yours, or generational) and onward

Above are just some examples of credit cards and points / savings system I have used in the past 20 years, for an estimated combined total savings of over $20,000 (including free flights and hotel stays).

If I considered this estimated $20,000 savings as part of my investment that compounds 7.2% annually, in the next 20 years, it has a potential to grow to more than $80,000.

Assuming I will continue to save at the same pace in the next 20 years, even if I did not invest any of the additional savings, the overall total free savings could amount to over $100,000.

And this is simply from free programs available to anyone, supplementing savings toward compounding growth.

For anyone that may think F.I.R.E. (financial independence; retire early) is not possible with family to support or with current income, I can tell you (now that I have actually reached the point where F.I.R.E. is an option) that, even if I had a lower income or a big family to take care of, my mindset and investment strategy would have allowed me to achieve a similar outcome, even if it took a few more years; it took me about 20 years since my early 20s, without being too frugal.

The reason I can say this with confidence, is because the wealth I accumulated by the time I turned 40 is from the compounding growth of money I had already invested in my 20s and early 30s (when my income was much lower), where I would have reached my current net worth without much additional investment in my late 30s or early 40s.

Although the amount of money each individual will need in order to consider themselves financially independent will vary depending on their lifestyle, with an open mind, a clear goal, consistent investment strategy, self-discipline, patience, and time, you will move forward no matter what.

Don't decide what you can or cannot do before you try.

If I was able to reach financial independence in about 20 years, based on what I know of what I spent on travel / entertainment over the years, and the many financial events / pullbacks I have been through over the years, it should be possible for many others.

It's never too late to start investing toward a more comfortable future (the earlier you start the better, but it's never too late to start), and doing something toward continuous improvement is definitely better than not doing anything.

What is "Financial Independence"

(Definition and timing of financial independence will depend on individual lifestyle needs, as well as life expectancy after retirement)

Cover ① ~ ⑧ for Financial Independence:

① List your living expense for each month, and choose the month with highest expense.

② Multiply ① times 12 for your overestimated annual living expense.

③ Multiply ① times 3 for your emergency fund (to be able to cover emergency medical bills, home/auto repairs, inflation, etc.).

④ Calculate the total annual cost of any recurring membership fees, taxes, and health/home/auto insurance (remember that private and company sponsored rates are different).

⑤ Add ②, ③ and ④ together.

⑥ Multiply ⑤ by the number of years you and your dependent expect to live after your retirement (multiplying with emergency fund included, is to intentionally overestimate for additional safety margin).

⑦ Invest half of ⑥ in index funds, a quarter in a no-risk high interest bank account, and the remaining quarter split between high potential investments and bonds.

⑧ Pay off your mortgage and other loans (or include in ① as part of monthly expense).

Why Millionaires Continue to Work

Possible reasons:

1. Majority of wealth is in retirement accounts (401k / IRA), which usually cannot be taken out without penalty until age 59.5, with a small portion of wealth in cash, properties, regular brokerage accounts, etc.; early withdrawal is an option, but will incur 10% penalty plus taxes and fees, which could result in hundreds of thousands of dollars wasted (~30% taken after taxes and fees).

2. Working to simply maintain health insurance (one of the greater benefits of working).

3. Working to build additional cash reserve (emergency fund to use whenever needed for the remainder of life).

4. Work is a passion in life (lucky few).

5. Work gives sense of accomplishment / purpose / responsibility (satisfaction from keeping busy, and feeling of being needed).

6. Pride.

7. To avoid boredom.

8. To check off a bucket list (in my case, I have always been interested in working at Costco to get insider knowledge on when best to shop, working at a lab, a book store, etc.).

There are likely various other reasons, and possibly combination of reasons why millionaires continue to work.

The idea is for everyone to be aware of the tools and mindset mentioned in this book, to reach the point where 'work' becomes an 'option'.

There are many other money saving and investing tips you can search online, including:

- VIX range vs. S&P500 trend
- Robo Advisor (AI investment)
- 4% rule / 3% rule
- Early Mortgage Payoff
- Home / Auto / Flood Insurance
  - o Reduce risk of loss
  - o Occasionally earn money from insurance
  - o Re-evaluate premiums at least once a year, etc.
  - o Ways of working with Adjuster / Contractor to maximize coverage and efficiency
- How to improve Credit Score
  - o To receive better rates
  - o Get better offers on credit cards, etc.
- Home Warranty Coverage
- Live and eat well for less
- DIY (and knowing when it is worth paying for service)
- Budgeting (using apps such as Mint and Personal Capital), etc.

Cover Photo Credit: NPS/Patrick Myers
Great Sand Dunes National Park - Mosca, Colorado

Made in the USA
Monee, IL
25 June 2023

37250686R00066